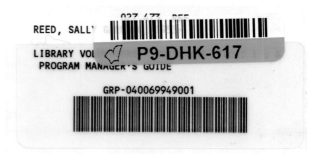
Library Volunteers — Worth the Effort!

In memory of
Mary McDermott, Barbara van de Velde,
and Phyllis Fisher —
library volunteers *extraordinaire*

Library Volunteers— Worth the Effort!

A Program Manager's Guide

by
Sally Gardner Reed

McFarland & Company, Inc., Publishers
Jefferson, North Carolina, and London

Cover: Sample volunteer appreciation certificate, designed by Shelley Countryman and reprinted by permission.

A Note to the Reader

To avoid the awkward he/she pronoun, I have alternated the pronoun gender with each chapter. "She" is used in chapters 1, 3, and 5, and "He" is used in chapters 2 and 4.

British Library Cataloguing-in-Publication data are available

Library of Congress Cataloguing-in-Publication Data

Reed, Sally Gardner, 1953–
    Library volunteers—worth the effort! : a program manager's guide / by Sally Gardner Reed.
        p.   cm.
    Includes bibliographical references and index.
    ISBN 0-7864-0004-8 (sewn softcover : 55# alk. paper) ∞
    1. Volunteer workers in libraries—United States.   2. Public libraries—United States—Personnel management.   I. Title.
Z682.4.V64R44   1994
027.473—dc20   94-4568
                                                                 CIP

Manufactured in the United States of America

McFarland & Company, Inc., Publishers
    Box 611, Jefferson, North Carolina 28640

Contents

Introduction

Historically, volunteers have played an important role in the development of libraries across the country. The public library movement itself grew from the voluntary efforts of concerned citizens who, wishing to establish libraries in their communities, worked to get funding and support to make them a reality. Many libraries in their infancy were staffed entirely by volunteers and were dependent on voluntary contributions to keep them open. In time, paid staff replaced volunteers in the management of libraries and in the delivery of service, as cities and towns took over the responsibility to provide public funding.

In many libraries, volunteers continue to play an important role. Whether employing volunteers on a daily basis to provide support for staff and services or using them only on occasion (for the library book sale or for special fund raising campaigns, for example), few libraries thrive without their assistance and support.

It is interesting that although most librarians who actively utilize the services of volunteers espouse their value, many do not "manage" this resource in an active and conscientious way. Many libraries do not have active recruitment, training and development programs for their volunteer staffs. Instead, volunteers often come and go, filling in where most apparently needed, almost without thought and effort on behalf of the library itself.

By taking a new look at your approach to volunteers; by spending the time and effort necessary to develop a well-managed volunteer work force that includes aggressive recruitment and systematic placement, training, and development, the value of volunteer services for your library can be enhanced immeasurably.

There are, of course, those libraries that have not used volunteer services in the past. Many of these libraries feel they have managed fairly well without volunteers and have never even given the issue much thought. Others have actively discouraged the use

1

of volunteers, finding the effort to schedule, train and monitor their performance to be too time consuming.

Times are changing, however, and libraries of all types are finding that as their financial support is declining, demand for service is not only increasing but becoming more sophisticated — requiring greater use of technology and outside resources. All of this means an already busy staff is put under greater pressure to maintain their level of services to their patrons. While volunteers can not and should not make up for inadequate staffing, they can be used by existing staff to ease the burden of the daily workload, enabling them to perform their duties in a more efficient manner.

To believe that libraries can run just as well (or even better!) without volunteers is to ignore the full scope of their value. Volunteers give libraries far more than just their time. Volunteers provide a special kind of support that no staff alone can generate. They are truly the community's representatives and as such they can provide fresh perspectives on and insights into library services. They will be outspoken advocates of the library in the community, speaking with voices that are far more powerful and compelling than ours exactly because they speak for something they believe in enough to voluntarily invest their time and talents. In addition, the presence of volunteers in the library will provide moral support to overworked staffs who may sometimes feel that their work goes unnoticed and unappreciated.

In a broader perspective, it's easy to see that library volunteers are valuable for more than helping staff meet the day to day requirements of their jobs. It is difficult, if not impossible, to think of a single successful library building project that did not depend heavily on volunteer time and services. It is equally hard to imagine that any kind of capital campaign could be successful without the hours of time and the expertise donated by various community members. Indeed, libraries that enjoy the financial support of Friends groups are indebted to the volunteers that comprise that group.

Public libraries are not alone in the debt they owe to volunteers. Many school libraries were established because parents recognized the value of having a library in support of the school's curricula and then worked hard to get them started. Today, many school libraries still depend on volunteer services from students, parents, and other community members for such routine tasks as staffing circulation desks, covering books, typing booklists, and putting together school library newsletters. While it is unfortunately true that in some cases (most notably in California), school administrators have justified the removal of librarians from school libraries on the grounds that they can be run by volunteers, it is far more often the case that volunteers in school libraries are a valuable resource for librarians who work hard to provide students with high quality professional library service.

Academic and special libraries have been least likely to use the services of volunteers but many are beginning to realize that they, too, can enhance their ability to serve their patrons by using volunteers. Not only that, but they are finding that student volunteers gain as well from the experience that work in the library can bring and some are beginning to actively recruit and develop student volunteer work forces.

According to the U.S. Bureau of Labor Statistics (as reported in *Monthly Labor Review*, February 1991, pages 17–23), approximately 20 percent of all Americans age 16 and over volunteer their time at least once during the course of a year. This impressive statistic is good news for libraries. Clearly, we see volunteer service as enriching us. Libraries are enriched by volunteer services and have been from the start. Just as the early libraries were dependent, at least in part, on the efforts of volunteers, many libraries continue to owe much of their vitality to volunteer assistance and support.

Librarians who recognize volunteers as valuable resources will continue to develop and manage their volunteer staffs as carefully and conscientiously as they do all their employees. Welcoming volunteers in the library and supporting them in all aspects of their employment will ensure that the volunteer services your library receives are the very best that they can be. In the end, everyone — staff members, volunteers, and patrons alike — will benefit from your efforts.

1

Why Volunteers?

The Standard Objections

No library that I know of suffers from a glut of personnel or is able to stay ahead of service demands consistently, or even keep up with them all on a day to day basis. Given that volunteers can provide free labor and assistance in accomplishing the myriad of library tasks that make up so much of each day, one might wonder why every library isn't actively recruiting and training all the volunteers it can find.

The reasons are simple. To begin with, those who are thinking about creating an active volunteer force may feel reluctance because of an ample supply of horror stories relating to the management of volunteers who bring with them differing levels of talent, commitment, team spirit, and available time. In fact, it is often those who have already created an active volunteer force who are relating the horror stories.

In addition, many librarians are concerned that by establishing a volunteer workforce they will be eliminating the need for paid assistance — something that could have detrimental long term effects on the library. Then, too, volunteers take a significant amount of training for the typically few hours per week they they work and often not as dependable as paid staff.

Given the very special effort it takes to create, manage and maintain a viable volunteer work force, it makes sense to ask the obvious — "Is it worth it?" From my perspective the answer is a resounding *YES!* There are good reasons to consider using volunteers and spending the time and effort necessary to ensure that their services are meaningful. Perhaps the most compelling reason, aside from the very obvious advantage of getting the extra help that libraries almost always need, is that volunteers can play an important role in your community and government relations.

People who volunteer to give time are exhibiting *prima facie* evidence of their support for the library. The opportunity to become involved in the delivery of library service will only enhance their commitment and increase their loyalty to the library, making them articulate advocates on the library's behalf. As active supporters of library services their voices will carry a good deal of weight because they will not be perceived by the local government as having self interest. It will be clear that they are backing their support in a very tangible way with the gift of their time and service.

As to those horror stories, believe them—they are probably all true; every volunteer manager has at least one story that can make you shudder. Managed appropriately, however, a good volunteer force will ease the burden of your staff, lift your spirits with their support, speak out on the library's behalf when you need them, and bring to the library new and innovative ideas for service. Because of the unique challenges associated with successful management of volunteers, there will probably always be the occasional "problem volunteer" or sensitive situation. By learning how to work with volunteers, however, to motivate and train them, to encourage and promote them, your library will reap rewards far greater than your level of effort.

The Threat to Paid Positions

Despite the enthusiasm with which some librarians support the use of volunteers, there are those who have firmly decided not to use volunteers and support that decision with some pretty strong reasoning. The first reason often heard is that by using volunteers, an inadequately staffed library will spend its best bargaining chip for getting the financial support it needs to increase personnel. In recognition of this concern, you will often hear the admonishment that volunteers should never be used to perform tasks that staff could be paid to do.

If you think about it, *any* task a volunteer does *could* be hired out. If the task is so unworthy that you wouldn't think about paying someone to do it, it probably isn't worth your time and effort in training to have a volunteer do it either. I agree, however, that a library would never want to disguise a need for more staffing by filling staff positions with volunteers. One colleague of mine refers to visible need for increased library support as the "pothole approach." No city will ever be motivated to spend precious resources on filling potholes if concerned citizens get out there and fill them themselves. Not only will money for filling potholes be hard to get if there is no visible problem, but concerned citizens are unlikely to have the skill necessary to fill potholes well enough to provide a somewhat lasting solution. Our visible (and unmet) needs, contends this colleague, are our potholes. We don't want to attempt to meet these needs with concerned citizens who often don't have the skills to do the job properly. As with the pothole metaphor, if the job is done by amateurs, it not only reduces our chance to get funding, but the quality of the job itself suffers, creating a definite decline in service delivery.

So, what is the response to those who are rightly concerned that volunteers might render a genuine need for more staff invisible? Simply this; volunteers should never be used to *replace* paid staff (or to fill a vacancy that was normally filled by a paid staff member) and that volunteers should not be used to perform ongoing jobs that require special skills or talents that would require another volunteer with similar expertise if she were to leave. This means that volunteer jobs should be somewhat generic. You don't want your level of service to decline because you handed a job over to a special volunteer with the unique qualifications needed to handle it and who then resigned leaving you with no other specially qualified volunteers available and no money to hire someone with those qualifications.

This does not apply, of course, to those very special or limited term tasks. If you are seeking volunteers for a special finite project, for example, you may actually recruit volunteers with specific and perhaps hard to find talents. A special project, such as a major fundraising drive, for example, may prompt you to seek out a volunteer with fundraising experience or one with marketing skills to help make the campaign a success.

There are other special needs that will require the special talents that not just any volunteer will be able to provide. You may seek out a member of your community, for example, who has outstanding graphic art talent to help you design a new library logo. You may look for a special volunteer with talents in calligraphy for producing promotional materials. You may have the need for a volunteer who can act as a translator for a new, non–English speaking family that has recently immigrated to the United States and has moved into your community.

While volunteers can certainly enhance your staff and their ability to deliver service, they should never be used in exchange for the regular staff you need. Even though it is true that volunteers typically take on jobs that someone could be hired to do, it makes sense to ensure that volunteer jobs support the work of your paid staff—jobs that enable your staff to be more productive and to enhance and expand their current level of service to the public.

Accountability

Another very good reason that libraries resist the idea of using volunteers is that they can present some unique challenges in personnel management. Perhaps chief among them is the difficulty in holding volunteers accountable for the quality of their work. No matter how theoretically correct it may sound to treat volunteers as you would paid employees, the simple fact is that they are not paid and that simple fact can make quite a difference when the quality of performance comes into question.

As unpleasant as it may be to correct and criticize the work of a substandard employee, criticizing the quality of the work of a volunteer can be especially difficult. Underlying every manager/ volunteer relationship is the unspoken but omnipresent reality that this worker is giving a gift of her time to the library. No one wants to be in the position of telling someone that her gift is far less than expected, that it isn't as valuable as the volunteer might think — that in fact, the "gift" is actually a burden because the volunteer is requiring too much supervision and her work is requiring too much retrospective adjustment.

When you have an employee who isn't measuring up to minimum performance standards and you have done all the coaching and remedial training possible, you begin progressive discipline. The employee knows that if her performance doesn't improve, she will lose her paycheck—the very thing that makes employees accountable. The volunteer, of course, receives no paycheck. While it makes sense to use coaching and remedial training as methods to get performance up to par, the use of progressive discipline will certainly be counterproductive. If progressive discipline is used with a well-meaning but low-functioning volunteer, the only losers are likely to be you and the library who will suffer from the very negative community relations and perhaps even in-house volunteer-relations that will result.

Even though the reality of volunteer management does differ from that of paid staff management, it need not be such an overwhelming obstacle that it prevents you from hiring volunteers at all. Proper placement and training of volunteers (see Chapters 2 and 3) will eliminate many volunteer performance problems before they even begin. The start of any volunteer's "employment" is the best chance you will ever have of imparting your library's philosophies and values. This is the time to make it very clear exactly what is expected of each volunteer and how her performance will be evaluated. By using written position descriptions, you will be able to spell out exactly your minimum requirements for productivity, for service, regularity of attendance, minimum number of hours per week or month, and reliability. If you are honest and clear at the start, your performance standards will be seen as objective and you will depersonalize to a great extent any future evaluations — even those that may be critical.

It is true that some volunteers are poor performers and it is also true that no amount of coaching, supervision, and remedial training will change that. But let's put this potential problem into perspective. *Most* volunteers are fine performers — don't abandon the idea of an important program because *some* volunteers are problems. Remember, too, that many if not most volunteer performance problems can be circumvented if volunteers are placed in positions that require very low levels of skill and then "promoted" as their talent and reliability dictates.

If what you require is more than a particular volunteer is willing to give, you are both better off finding that out before the volunteer is brought on board. If you agree to minimum standards from the beginning and are very clear about what they are, it is much easier to talk about performance slippage because you have a clearly identified set of standards against which to measure her performance. This kind of objectivity makes criticism and evaluation so much easier for both of you—in fact, this setting of clear expectations should be used with *all* your employees.

They're Just More Trouble Than They're Worth

A friend of mine is the circulation manager at her public library which carries with it the role of volunteer coordinator. She told me that her library was interviewing candidates for the position of library director and part of the process included interviews with the existing library staff. During the course of the staff interview, candidates were asked how they felt about volunteers in the library.

One candidate blithely responded that it is a pretty well accepted fact that volunteers require much more training and supervision than the average staff member and in fact, the amount of time it takes to manage a volunteer staff far outweighs any contribution that volunteers might make. He summed up, "They're just more trouble than they're worth."

"Right then and there," my colleague told me, "I knew he was out of the running." In further explanation, she said that for the staff and her, this comment spoke volumes about the candidate's management acumen, not to mention his sensitivity in speaking disparagingly about volunteers to staff members who fully support volunteers in the workplace as evidenced by their large and diverse volunteer workforce.

It is a common belief that the management of volunteers does take more time and effort than the management of paid staff—and this belief is, on the whole, undoubtedly true. Volunteers work less frequently than paid staff and are, therefore, more prone to mistakes. Furthermore, for most volunteers, work at the library is just one aspect of a busy life. For most, volunteer work at the library is not the focal point of their lives the way jobs often are for paid workers. Their level of commitment may not be less, necessarily, but it may well be limited to those relatively few hours the volunteer dedicates out of her week to the library.

So the question arises, does the added training, monitoring, and supervision that many volunteers require negate their value to the library? Not if the volunteer has been placed in a position commensurate with her talent. Not if the volunteer receives the initial training necessary to do the job well over the long haul. Not if the volunteer receives the support along the way to develop the self-confidence necessary to grow and become independent in her position. All of this, you will notice, puts the responsibility for good volunteer performance squarely on the shoulders of *management* and that is why, in a nutshell, the candidate who felt volunteers "weren't worth the trouble" was immediately seen as a poor choice for the position of library director.

Yes, volunteers may take some more time and attention than paid staff but, again, it's a matter of perspective. If managed correctly, volunteers can give so much back in terms of time and support. Ask any busy staff member, whose load is lightened each week by a volunteer who comes in to take on some of the more menial chores associated with her job, if volunteers are worth the trouble. If volunteers are carefully placed according to their abilities, if they understand up front exactly what is required of them, if they get lots of positive feedback and reinforcement, the extra time and "trouble" it takes to manage volunteers can pay the library back many times over, and in many different ways.

Putting the Objections in Perspective

The concerns about the use of volunteers in libraries are valid but they need not be overwhelming to the extent that they discourage the use of volunteers altogether. Volunteers need not and should not replace paid staff, that's true. But think about it. How many libraries have all the paid staff they need? In fact, have libraries *ever* had all the paid staff they need? Even if a library is running quite smoothly with all tasks being accomplished easily and in a timely manner, there are always opportunities to expand and improve services—doing so almost always means extra work for staff members—extra work that could easily be made more manageable with the assistance of volunteers.

Accountability of volunteers is different than that of paid staff members. Hours may be more irregular and vacations more frequent. If you are not using volunteers in place of paid staff, however, this factor should not be so important. By understanding that volunteers only augment staff, you will be far more flexible with regard to volunteer hours. And while it's also true that holding volunteers accountable for the same quality of work as paid employees is not really possible, you can find tasks that are important and necessary that require very little talent or expertise making this kind of accountability far less important.

It's true, it does take a lot of time and effort to train and maintain a volunteer workforce. It's easy to see, then, why volunteers may be perceived to come at a price too dear—especially for libraries that lack the available personnel to do the kind of thorough training and supervising necessary to ensure that the volunteer *can* meet expectations. Paradoxically, the library that might benefit most from the services of volunteers are often those least likely to feel they have the time to create an effective volunteer force. If you are hesitating to use volunteers because you don't have the staff time necessary to adequately manage them, consider making a strong case for that added staff member. Local government leaders who ultimately decide the library's budget may be easily convinced to add one staff member when it means that the library will be able to get hundreds or thousands of volunteer hours each year as a result.

With good management, volunteers will definitely mean a net gain in the number of "people hours" you have available to deliver library service to your community. Once you have a good corp of volunteers coming in to help the library in the accomplishment of its many goals, you'll wonder how you ever got along before with them.

Good Reasons for Using Volunteers

Help!

The most important reason for developing and nurturing a strong and active volunteer force is to get the help you need to meet the library's goals for service. It's probably true that in most towns and cities, residents use their public library more frequently than any other municipal service agency. In fact, we know that as the economy declines, use of public libraries typically increases. Just when we need more money for more staff to meet increasing demand, the lagging economy is used by municipal leaders as an excuse to reduce their level of library support.

Even if libraries work to accommodate insufficient budgets by reducing or eliminating various programs, the basic services we offer for information retrieval and the loaning of materials is extremely labor intensive and the demands put upon us for these two most basic of library services can be the most difficult to meet with insufficient staff. Even a reduction in hours only means a greater intensity of demand for the staff during the hours the library is open.

Often, to meet the basic needs of our patrons, professional staff are called upon to accomplish some clerical duties, and clerks and assistants are so busy meeting the public that many of their tasks are put on the "back burner" where sometimes they stay indefinitely—slowly eroding the quality of service the library is able to give.

Volunteers are perfect for taking up some of the slack that gets neglected or delayed by staff members whose first priority must be to serve the patron in front of them. Without requiring special talents or skills, it is usually possible to find people in the community who will be willing to shelve books, do simple filing and typing, check the accuracy of and send overdue notices, cover books, collect discarded materials from tables and chairs—the list is endless. I'm not talking about replacing paid staff, I'm talking about volunteers who can assist the staff you have and enable them to get their jobs done and done well.

If your library is lucky enough to be well staffed and all back burners are empty, volunteers are a wonderful resource for *expanding* the programs that you currently offer. Few libraries, if any, are in a position to feel completely complacent, and if there are such libraries, the changing world necessitates changing library services. Volunteers can make the development and implementation of new programs possible and even easy.

Unless a new program is replacing an old program, there will be additional work for the staff. And, if a new program proves to be as popular and successful as you hope, work will certainly follow. Existing staff can often cope well with expanding and changing services—it's in the nature of the job. Morale, however, will surely suffer if no support is put in place to help them accommodate changing job requirements.

Sometimes service changes are so significant and "permanent" that a case can and should be made for additional staff to support the changes. In fact, I would argue that it would be irresponsible for a library to take on major, labor-intensive programs or services of a permanent nature without ensuring that additional staff are available to support the change. Librarians, being in the business of providing public service, often find it hard to say no. Unfortunately, our funders usually find saying "no" very easy indeed. The cost to libraries, then, of expanding programs without financial support is low morale and a decline in the quality of service we are able to provide.

Modifications in service, however, and gradual increases in the levels of service can often be handled well if volunteers are available to support staff in the delivery of these services. Again, by acting as *support* to library staff, they can ease the load by taking care of much of the time-consuming, menial tasks that comprise so much of our work. Volunteers, in fact, may help you get a trial program off the ground the subsequent success of which may be just the ammunition you need to convince policy makers that the library matters, is popular, and should be fully funded.

Fresh Perspectives

Though you may not recruit volunteers for the fresh perspectives and new insights they can bring to your library, the fact is they can and will! Volunteers often make up the greatest diversity on staff in terms of background, education, and beliefs. How fortunate for you to have this wide range of viewpoints at your disposal.

The truth is, we librarians are a pretty in-bred lot. We tend to learn from each other, discuss our management problems with one another, attend conferences with one another, and seek solutions and innovations from each other. While all this is basically okay, it can certainly be limiting. Many library managers are actively applying general management and marketing principles developed *outside* the library and when they do, they often find that innovation and a refreshed spirit is introduced into the library.

Despite taking a broad management view, most libraries are still developing their direction and vision from their own (that is, library) perspective. Even if we survey our communities and include honest and open dialogue with community members as part of our self-evaluations, those surveys and dialogues are still likely to be strongly colored by our own perspective. The questions we ask, the frameworks we design for discussion, will all come from the issues and services *we* have identified as important.

Because so much of what we do and how we do it is influenced by those on staff—those delivering library service, it can only benefit the library to include among them people who come from outside the library world, people whose interests and commitments are broad and include libraries only as one of many interests. When you have people contributing to library service who are not enmeshed in traditional library methods, values, and traditions, you are likely to get very innovative perspectives on what you do and how you are doing it.

Granted, many ideas about service delivery coming from people who have relatively uninformed perspectives will be, well, a little crazy. Some ideas will be too expensive and some completely impractical. In some cases, ideas presented by volunteers will be in direct conflict with important library principles and philosophies.

I had a volunteer once who was committed to the idea of buying the city parking lot adjacent to our building. For that initial investment, he insisted that we could charge patrons (and even staff—I'm not kidding!) enough to pay for the lot in a few short years at which time we would begin to generate extra revenue for the library. The suggestion may have made sense from a financial point of view, but it certainly would violate our commitment to access. Despite my reasoning against such a plan, I must confess that this volunteer remained forever unconvinced. He maintained that everyone was used to paying for parking and that the charge would be nominal enough so that anyone could pay. Even though I refused to budge on this idea, I did let the volunteer know that his kind of creative and innovative thinking is valued even if there were ideas that would not be adopted as practice.

In among the plethora of new ideas for library service and the delivery of service that just are not tenable, however, you will find the occasional "crazy" idea that just might work. Innovation so often comes from the outside; from superimposing unlikely possibilities on traditional practices. People who are not as caught up in the library world as we who work for them on a daily basis are often just the people to see those possibilities.

If you doubt the confining nature of your traditional perspectives, you can test yourself by trying to solve the well known puzzle below.

Connect the nine dots below using four straight connected lines (solution on page 18).

If you haven't seen this puzzle before, it is likely that you set limitations for yourself that hampered your ability to solve it. If you're already familiar with the puzzle and its solution, you might still consider it a reminder that sometimes new perspective is just what's needed to find solutions.

Community Representatives

Because we serve the community, we put a lot of effort into trying to determine what the community's needs for service are. The entire planning process revolves around the concept of community needs. We spend time and effort in ascertaining those needs and in developing ways to meet them. Finally, we design and fight for budgets that are driven by what we understand the community's needs for library service to be. Being responsive to the community is foundational for good library service.

Most honest librarians will admit that our understanding of what the public wants and needs from its library and the public's own perception often differs—sometimes dramatically. For example, while many public libraries have banked on the belief that what the public wants most is popular reading material ready and available *when* they want it, reality has shown that in fact even though readily available best-sellers and popular books are, well, *popular* with many library users, these very users don't necessarily view such service as *important* or even necessary—at least when money is tight. Libraries that weather poor economic times best are those whose services are as strongly diverse as the community itself;

libraries that have focused on more "indispensable" community needs as job hunting support, literacy programs, children's services, reference services, and community information services—those services that the entire community considers important.

We have ways of determining what the community's needs for service are and we have found that some are less than effective. For example, many libraries have used circulation statistics to determine that best-sellers are what the public wants most. But circulation statistics don't tell the whole story and can even be misleading if we depend upon them too heavily.

An interesting study done by George D'Elia, professor at the Carlson School of Management, University of Minnesota, Minneapolis, showed that what the 1,000 citizens surveyed nationally by Gallup wanted most from their public library was *not* popular reading as I am sure many of their own libraries had determined. Four out of the top five roles identified as important by those surveyed had to do with the provision of information and support for education—both formal and independent. Rounding out the top five most important roles, was that of support for preschoolers' learning. Popular reading was viewed as the most important role only 50 percent of the time and ranked sixth out of eight role choices. And how was this discrepancy discovered? Not by a look at the statistics, but by asking people individually how important they found various library services (*Library Journal*, August, 1992, page 16).

Frequent library users who enjoy best-selling works often check out far more books than the average library user and that inflates the circulation figures for those books. It is hard, if not impossible, to measure the value a patron gets from using materials in-house, getting an answer to a reference question, finding a place for quiet study, or coming in to make contact with others who have similar interests in the meeting room, against those who check out armfuls of books each week using numbers alone. If you do, you are not likely to come up with an honest picture of how the community at large views the relative importance of your services.

Like D'Elia's study above, sometimes the best information comes from communicating with members of the community themselves. Who better to give you feedback on the quality and effectiveness of your services as seen by those you serve than your volunteers who you've recruited from all segments of your community? Your volunteers are your conduits to the community. Their

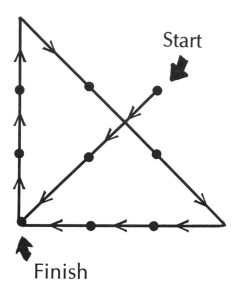

Start

Solution to puzzle on page 16

Finish

lives are not likely to revolve around library work and because, typically, they spend only a few hours a week in the library, they have time to pursue other interests. What all of this means for the library is that collectively, they are more involved in the community in a wider variety of ways than you and your staff. They will bring to their volunteer work not only their own fresh perspectives, but the perspectives of others in their lives with whom they talk about their work at the library.

In order to tap into this valuable information, it makes sense to communicate with volunteers on a regular basis. Actively solicit information and feedback from them by asking them direct questions about what they see as the strengths and weaknesses in library service. Hold volunteer staff meetings not only to bring volunteers up to date with what is happening at the library but also to get information from them. What are people telling them about the library's services? What have they observed themselves? Consider placing a suggestion box in an area where all your volunteers have easy access to it and encourage them to be regular contributors.

Finally, don't overlook the valuable contribution volunteers can make in the planning process. When you develop staff committees to relook at the library's mission, to set goals and to analyze current service; be sure that you have some of your volunteers working on those committees, too. They will tell you how the library is perceived out there. They will know which services are generally supported and which are questioned, misunderstood, or criticized. It's important information—information that people will talk about with each other but perhaps won't share with library staff who are proud of what they provide, even if it's something no one else considers all that important. It's information that doesn't always show up in the statistics.

Library Advocates

Perhaps the most important contribution a volunteer makes is relatively inadvertent. Volunteers are our best direct links to the community. They are "one of them" as opposed to being "one of us." When volunteers talk of their work in the library to their friends and neighbors they are speaking out on our library's behalf. When they defend the library's need for funding to the people in their lives, their voices carry weight. First of all, they should know—they work for the library. And even more important, they are seen by everyone as part of the funding solution. Volunteers are not just paying taxes (and willing to pay more for library support), they are giving their time and effort to help libraries deliver those services that they support.

If volunteers are effective advocates simply by talking about their library work in their own circles without any coaching from us, imagine how effective they could be with our encouragement and support. The best library advocates are those who are well informed, who have the facts about service and financial needs, and who are actively encouraged to speak out in the community. The volunteers who know the most about library operations and who understand best the role a library plays in the community are the volunteers who can be most articulate and persuasive.

There are many ways in which the library can work to empower volunteers to be effective ambassadors and they all have to do with good communication from the library. Consider, for example, including volunteers in your regular staff meetings. While it's true that time could be an important constraint for the volunteers who work only a couple hours a week, by inviting or encouraging them to come at least once in awhile, you'll be sending the message that they matter to you and that you view them as an important component of your staff. In addition, by attending a staff meeting now and then, a volunteer will get a clearer understanding of the issues facing the library on a daily basis and how the staff works together to solve problems and increase the quality and effectiveness of its service.

Libraries with large volunteer staffs would do well to consider a volunteer newsletter—one that is designed and published by the volunteers themselves. A volunteer newsletter is a great way to ensure that members of a volunteer staff who have little interaction with one another—and often little interaction with the staff as a whole, will stay well informed about matters that pertain especially to them. Changes in volunteer requirements, volunteer job openings in the library, a monthly accounting of volunteer hours donated to the library, a reminder that suggestions by volunteers are welcome, announcements of upcoming volunteer events and library programs of interest are all important communiques. In addition, a volunteer newsletter is a great way to ensure that you don't leave anyone out of the information loop.

If you have established a volunteer newsletter, you can work with its editor to include articles about important library issues. Your volunteers should know about such things as changes in policies, requests for additional funding, and plans for expansion. What's more, volunteers should understand *why* the library administration is making these decisions, requests or plans. If volunteers understand and support your plans, they will be able to explain and defend them successfully to those in their lives who are bound to question them.

Once you've ensured that volunteers are well-informed, it makes sense to let them know that they do play an ambassador role for the library by virtue of their unique relationship to it. Prevail upon them to be active advocates and give them the support, encouragement, and training they need to do it well. Most libraries take time throughout the year to bring the volunteer staff together to discuss changes in policy and practice and to discuss issues relating to their work. Why not expand those meetings to discuss as well why libraries are important and the contribution both the volunteer and the library makes to the community? Having a well articulated philosophical foundation underpinning their natural love of libraries will better prepare them to be effective advocates.

Once volunteers are aware of and comfortable with their auxiliary role as library ambassadors, you can talk with them about ways to be more aggressive in that role. A diverse group of volunteers will have a diversity of interests in their lives. Many will belong to other groups and organizations in the community groups that might be in a position to help the library. Most volunteers are doers. If they are giving some of their time to the library, it's entirely possible that they are spending some of their time with other organizations as well. Volunteers who are members of service organizations and social clubs such as Rotary, Y.W.C.A., Kiwanis, the local garden club, for example, can be unofficial library spokespeople within those groups. Those who are active in political organizations can tout the library to their leaders increasing the library's clout in that particular arena. Volunteers who work for other service agencies will be able to promote the library's services to those agencies and may discover compatible goals which could open the door to opportunities for resource and idea sharing.

Networking and coalition building does not need to (and shouldn't) reside solely in the administrative purview. Volunteers can help build effective coalitions for the library and because they come from a variety of backgrounds, their influence is bound to be far reaching.

That volunteers can be effective advocates is not a revolutionary notion. The most successful campaigns I know of for increased or maintained library support, for example, have relied heavily on the services of volunteers — and in these cases, there was nothing inadvertent about it! For all the reasons that volunteers are effective advocates to their friends, families and affiliations, they make extremely effective advocates to policy makers. The fact is, because their opinions have been formed by their working knowledge of the library's operations, they better than most clearly understand the library's needs. Not only that but volunteers have the virtue of actually making a difference in giving their time to the library. Their role as advocates is indeed enhanced by the important fact that they will not be viewed by policy makers as having self-interest.

A librarian's fight for financial support is certainly informed but it will also be seen as self-interested. Despite the fact that librarians work hard to provide an important and popular service, they will always be seen by city management as protecting turf if they are unwilling to suffer cuts gladly and they will often be seen as kingdom builders by policy makers who, despite all our best efforts, fail to grasp the importance of the library in their community.

Even trustees who are very often appointed by the policy makers they try to persuade in the fight for library support, will be seen as self-interested. By the very virtue of their positions, they have a vested interest in the library. Sadly, rather than being seen as informed community representatives, their voices are often weakened in the eyes of government by the very positions they were elected or appointed to fill.

Volunteers also have a vested interest in the library. The library is, after all, an institution that they care enough about to give their time. The very act of giving their time, however, will cast them in the light of commitment that goes beyond self interest. Local officials understand very well how important volunteer services are to the smooth running and enrichment of city services. When volunteers speak out on behalf of libraries, officials will listen because they, like us, are beholden to volunteers.

It's important to realize, too, that when the library utilizes the services of volunteers our credibility is enhanced when we claim that we are doing everything possible with resources available to maintain quality library service. In a subtle but important way, the very fact that so many community members are willing to volunteer their time to the library sends the message that the library matters — after all, how many people volunteer for work in the city manager's office?

From Advocate to Activist

Being a library advocate and being a library activist are two important, but very different roles. While you encourage and hope that all your volunteers will be good advocates all the time, there will occasionally be those special times when you need to turn those advocates into active lobbyists for library support.

Whether planning a campaign for a significant increase in your budget, making a case to ward off a devastating cut, or working to get the money you need for a new or expanded facility, you will need a lot of people in your corner — not just lending moral support but actively working to ensure that the library gets the money it needs.

No major campaign will be successful unless you have strong grassroots support and the volunteers just happen to be the best representatives you have on board representing the grassroots. Their commitment is already demonstrated by the fact that they are giving their time to the library, and if you've done a good job of keeping them informed about library issues and informed about ways in which they can garner general library support and good will in the community, the step of turning volunteers into activists is a very short one.

The time always comes when the library must convince city government of a need for special or increased funding or to convince the entire community (as when you are trying to pass a bond issue). When that time comes, volunteers can be your best lobbyists. In convincing government of the library's need they can speak strongly and intelligently as community representatives. In the battle to gain a majority vote in your community, they can take on the enormous work that will be involved in ensuring a successful outcome.

Too often, libraries are seen by local government as an auxiliary community service; nice but not essential. This perception can be especially devastating when the economy is suffering or when local governments are dealing with a tax-payer revolt— whether the revolt has been translated into mandated tax caps or just the threat of such a mandate is present. When city funding officials decide to tighten their belts, any service that they perceive to be pleasant but periphery is endangered.

The future health of library funding is in the hands of policy makers who must come to appreciate the importance of libraries— importance that increases when the economy declines. Our profession has recognized this fact and strong efforts have been made to show the significance of libraries to those who are in a position to harm or help us. These efforts, however, will never succeed unless the importance of libraries is tied to people. Policy makers and government officials are elected by people and even if they never fully appreciate the value of libraries, they can be held accountable to their constituency.

It is no secret that people wield the greatest influence at the local level. That's good news for your library because people power is just exactly what you have—beginning with your volunteers. There is likely to be a time (unfortunately, it's likely to happen more than once) when a librarian's case for critical funding needs are not supported by local government. Even with the full weight of the Board behind the request, facts alone can be ineffective in persuading government officials. If they are not convinced that libraries are a priority service, even predictions of service cuts and layoffs are unlikely to change their minds. What will? The voices of those who voted them into office.

Volunteers can make up the core of a powerful network of community support. Major funding battles should not be waged alone. If your needs are critical, get help from those who will most directly benefit from your success or be deprived by your failure to secure adequate library funding. Your volunteers can speak out at council meetings about the important role the library plays in the community. What's more, volunteers can appeal to their friends and neighbors, to their colleagues and associates, to their local representatives making the case for library funding.

Elected officials need to know what the consequences of their actions will be if library funding is cut or not appropriated at sufficient levels to meet the needs of the community. The librarian can tell them and so can the Board of Trustees. But again, our voices are weakened by the perception of our self-interest. Volunteers are diverse, they are the public, they are the voters, they are the grassroots. It makes sense to get them working actively on the library's side to generate phone calls and letters to those in government who can help libraries or hurt them.

If volunteers are important in convincing government that libraries must be fully funded, they are absolutely indispensable in convincing the community at large to support the library at the ballot box. Here's where you can really put a strong volunteer force to work for the library. The library staff can do a lot to convince the community to support special funding, but the kind of involvement we have in making the case will be scrutinized by the public and criticized by our detractors if it looks like we are spending valuable city time "campaigning."

Librarians will be most effective in *informing* the public: letting individual citizens and groups know *why* the money is needed, exactly how it will be used, and what the consequences will be if funding is not forthcoming. There is a thin line between this kind of education and doing what might look like campaigning. It's a line that is well worth our efforts to pay attention to. Any "vote yes" literature should come from volunteers and be clearly labeled as such. Many will be quick to see a breach of ethics in using city money (whether directly for campaign literature, or indirectly for staff time) and it will weaken the library's case.

Volunteers in your library augmented by those who have been specially recruited by the Friends of the Library or the Board of Trustees are the ones who can energetically and unequivocally make the case for the library. It will often be necessary to go beyond providing citizens with information and education they need to make an intelligent decision about the library's needs. There will be times when it is necessary to actively work to get the vote out and to do everything possible to persuade voters that their ballots should be cast in favor of the library—your volunteers are just the ones to do it.

Volunteers—Definitely Worth the "Trouble"

Do volunteers generally take extra time to train? Are they often more prone to mistakes than paid staff? Is it harder to hold them accountable for the quality of their work? Are they worth the trouble? Almost any librarian who has set up and maintains an active volunteer workforce will tell you that the answer to all these questions is yes. They can take more time and more management skill but they are definitely worth it.

Volunteers have so much to offer besides the obvious benefit of additional people to tackle the seemingly never ending work involved in delivering library service. Volunteers can be effective community representatives who can carry communication two ways. They can tout and explain library services and policies to the people in their lives, and they can provide excellent feedback from the community on how well the library is doing. Best of all, the larger your volunteer force, the larger your core group of library lobbyists. No library can afford to work in a vacuum. No library is better off without the input and support of community members. Welcome volunteers for all that they can do to enhance library service—their ability to do so effectively is really up to us.

2

Recruitment and Placement
of Volunteers

If you're lucky, you have a steady stream of able and energetic people of all ages and backgrounds coming into your library to offer their assistance as volunteers. If yours is like most libraries, however, you don't have all the volunteers you need and the volunteers you do get tend to be from the same age group (retired), the same cultural background (white, middle-class), and are primarily female. While there is nothing at all wrong with this group—they form the backbone of volunteer services across the country—they do represent a fairly narrow segment of any community's population and aren't representative of the rich diversity that surrounds us.

Because volunteers *do* enable libraries to reflect community diversity in a very visible way, and because people with different backgrounds and lifestyles bring a richness of talent and perspective, it makes sense to make a real effort at bringing in volunteers from all walks of life. In addition to that core of people who seek out volunteer opportunities, you'll do your library a real favor by actively working to swell your volunteer ranks.

It's possible that if your library has not traditionally used volunteers or encouraged their services, you may not have even a trickle of interest that comes without bidding. Unless your library receives a large and steady supply of diverse volunteers right off the street, you'll find that you must go out into the community to encourage greater interest in the library's volunteer program.

Where to Find Volunteers

When you start thinking about the different kinds of people you'd like to see working in the library, you'll also begin to get ideas about where to find them. Identifying interests of various groups of people who might like to give some time to the library will provide you with just the clues you need to seek them out and appeal to them in terms of their own interests. To increase the diversity of the volunteer staff and the variety of talents and perspectives they might bring, think about the different characteristics that make up your community's profile.

Consider, for example, the ethnic and racial make-up of the community; how well is this make-up reflected in your volunteer staff? What about age? gender? lifestyle? background and occupation? In every community, no matter how homogenous it may appear on the surface, there are a variety of people who would bring significant richness, diversity and perspective to your library. And of course, the wider variety of people, the wider variety of talent you'll have available to you through your volunteers.

Service Clubs

A good place to begin in your active recruitment for volunteers is with local community service organizations and clubs. These places are naturals for volunteers because by definition, those belonging to service organizations are interested in improving the quality of life for their communities. You will be preaching to the choir when you explain the library's need for volunteers and it is likely that many members of these groups will be very interested in volunteer opportunities at the library.

Perhaps the one obstacle that you might face is that these people tend to be "doers." They've taken the personal initiative to join an organization that will put them to work. You may find that these people have already committed the bulk of their spare time to other projects—those initiated by their own organizations, for example. Even if you aren't successful in filling routine weekly spots in the library with volunteers you've recruited from service agencies, you might be able to get a few of those special projects off the back burner that will just take a few hours of someone's concerted effort.

Consider, too, the possibility of getting a large project accomplished by a group of volunteers on a one-time-only basis. For example, if the library's grounds need a major clean-up that might include patching sidewalks, clipping hedges, and painting the library's front door, you could ask the community garden club to take it on as a spring project. How about the Rotary Club or a local Boy Scout or Girl Scout troop?

If you are thinking of a big project, think big in terms of volunteers; many of these projects are tailor-made for groups which have formed for the very purpose of making a contribution to their community.

Schools

Many librarians and library employees began their careers volunteering for their school or public library. Not only do young people have a lot to offer as volunteers, you might be providing the first notion for some kids that a career in libraries would be a perfect choice for them. While it is undoubtedly true that teenaged volunteers often require more supervision and direction, they also have a lot to offer. Teenaged volunteers bring energy, enthusiasm, and let's face it . . . youth!

Public and school libraries across the country have successfully launched teen volunteer programs, often with a teen-advisory component. Teenagers are actively recruited to become more involved with all aspects of planning, programming, and selecting for the young adult room and for young adult services. When teens have some say in the development of services that they are interested in, they are much more likely to use the library. Many teenagers will love to have the opportunity to "work" at the library and it is surprising how much some have to contribute.

In addition to having a hand in planning their own services, teens can be exceptional volunteers in the children's room. Many teenagers have fond memories of their own experience with children's library services and are happy to volunteer to shelve picture books, work at the youth circulation desk, or to take part in planning and even implementing some programs for younger kids. A teen volunteer library council could be developed to put some children's programming together—telling stories or putting on a play, for example, would be very popular for teens and younger children alike.

If you are interested in getting younger people represented in your volunteer staff, contact your local high school guidance counselor or school media specialist to see what kind of placement service they provide for the community. Many high schools support and encourage community involvement by their students. If this is the case in your community, it is likely that you will be able to make contact with someone at the high school who will facilitate the placement of kids who have the appropriate skills and interests to work in the library (be careful that the school volunteer coordinator or counselor isn't harboring the old stereotype of libraries and feels compelled to send you nothing but shy, quiet bookworms—it's nice to have some of the outgoing, dynamic kids too!).

You should also find out if your local high schools have a job training program that seeks out opportunities in the community to provide students with job skills. Such programs often give students release time from classes to "work" in the community and the kids receive school credit for their efforts. Here again is another chance not only to get some volunteer help for the library, but to highlight librarianship as a viable career option for a student who is beginning to look to the future.

Local colleges and universities are also excellent sources for young and bright volunteers. Most have volunteer placement services and because students *choose* to participate in such programs, you can be assured of getting a student who is truly committed to public service and wants to make a meaningful contribution to the community.

Perhaps nowhere is a student body more diverse than at a community college. Because the curriculum is so varied, and because people of all ages and backgrounds are encouraged to participate in the community college's program, the student body is likely to have among its members anyone from a professional engineer polishing his word processing skills to a new immigrant learning English as a second language, to a middle aged woman wishing to enter the work force for the very first time. While it will probably be true that community college students are among the busiest (many will hold full-time jobs in addition to taking classes), there may be a program in place for on-the-job training and you might be able to get a student who is interested in becoming a library technician to volunteer for a semester while earning college credit for the experience.

All libraries can play an important role in mentoring "at risk" students who come from a variety of ethnic, racial, and economic backgrounds. One place to begin such a mentoring program (formally or informally) is through an active volunteer program for teens and young adults that welcomes and encourages diversity. If you also make it a policy to hire part-time or temporary help from this particular pool of volunteers, you will increase and maintain interest among these young people and you will provide them with a good possibility of part-time work as they progress through school.

When we look at the appallingly low numbers of nonwhite students in graduate school, we can see that equal opportunity is a pretty empty phrase for many people in our society. This gap in numbers between white and nonwhite graduate students has a dramatic and negative impact on our own profession and that impact will increase as more and more students enter our school system with ethnically and racially diverse backgrounds. Be visionary. Look at your teen and young adult volunteer program as a possible launch pad for students who are all too often left behind and who might, instead, become part of our own profession someday.

Volunteer Placement Agencies and "Special" Volunteers

Almost every community in the country has a volunteer placement agency such as Retired Seniors Volunteer Program (RSVP), Green Thumb, a chapter of the National Assistance League, Youth Efforts in Service (YES—which is another good avenue for bringing teen volunteers into the library, see above), or the local United Way. These agencies exist for the very purpose of placing interested members of the community in volunteer situations. Some agencies, such as RSVP, have a very well defined membership—in this case, retired persons. There may also be agencies that seek to place "displaced" members of the community or more "nontraditional" volunteers. If you are interested in bringing in a wide variety of volunteers, check with your local United Way office to find out which organizations in your city or town help place volunteers. You will likely find that there are people who for a variety of reasons have been out of the work force for some time and need the opportunity to brush up on their work skills. You will also find that there are "special needs" people in your community like those with learning handicaps who need the opportunity to be streamlined into the community through a work place.

While I would be the first to say that libraries do not exist to solve all the world's social needs, and that our very first priority should be to recruit volunteers who can be productive and whose supervision needs do not outweigh their ability to contribute, I believe that we often narrow opportunities to bring on valuable volunteers when we narrow our perspectives on who is able to make meaningful and useful contributions. If you have agencies that place "special" or "nontraditional" community members in volunteer situations you should talk to them. There is a wide variety of jobs in any library and the requirements to effectively do those jobs varies as well. You might find that you have just the right job for a person with limited job skills or who has physical or mental limitations.

I found out for myself that my own perception was more limited than the abilities of a particular young man in the community who was mentally retarded. Because his handicap was slight, Dan's advocate and supervisor was anxious to place Dan in a routine volunteer situation where he could learn some job skills, strengthen his sense of responsibility and build self-esteem. I was reluctant to place Dan because I was concerned that the oversight of his work would require too much time and effort from an already overworked staff. Dan's advocate, however, assured me that he would accompany Dan and work with him as he completed his weekly shift. We spent time training both Dan and his supervisor and true to his word, the supervisor came every time and worked right alongside Dan ensuring quality control. In fact, when Dan was unable to come in for his shift, his supervisor came alone to ensure that the assigned work would get done!

We found simple but important work for Dan. He began his shift by emptying the book drops, sorting children and adult materials for check-in. Dan then circled throughout the library collecting materials left behind on tables, shelves and carrels and returned them to the circulation desk for re-shelving. Dan stayed with the library for several years and the library was rewarded with a valued and well-liked member of the volunteer staff. In the end, Dan was rewarded with a real job that his new work skills enabled him to find, and his farewell note to me was my personal reward.

May 15, 1991

Mrs. Reed,

I'm sorry to say, but I've recently acquired a job which is from Tuesday through Friday from 10:30 to 2:30. Therefore, I will not be able to do my volunteer work here at the Isley Library anymore.

It's been a real pleaser working with you and the other staff members and you all will really be missed by myself.

Again, Thank You for the opportunity to be involved in such a nice atmosphere.

Sincerely yours,
Danny Keith Stokes

Court Diversion and Community Service

I've heard many librarians talk disparagingly about the library's being a "dumping ground" when it comes to people who need to fulfill a community service requirement. It's true, many if not most of these people are not the salt of the earth and not typically the type thought of as ideal library volunteers. But, before you dismiss the idea of using people assigned to do community service through court diversion, talk to your custodian or building supervisor.

Even if a person is not exactly the type you'd like serving the public, it is very possible that there are minor building projects that have been set aside for lack of time. It is often the case that those having to perform community service have many hours to devote in order to complete their sentences. It may be the perfect opportunity to get some interior painting done, windows washed, shelving throughout the building dusted and cleaned, and to accomplish the minor repair of furniture and equipment. The possibilities, at least from your custodian's point of view, are probably endless.

If you choose to take advantage of someone needing to fulfill a community service obligation, be sure to speak with his probation officer. Find out exactly what the person's crime was and be sure that he does not have a history of committing crimes or misdemeanors that could put library property or staff at risk. Also, be sure that the library staff member who will be supervising this person is completely comfortable with the idea of working with someone from court diversion and will be able to supervise the individual closely. It would be nice to give the miscreant a clean slate and reasonable trust, but in reality these people are not "volunteering" in the strictest sense of the word, they are under a bit of duress. Because you are managing the city's property and resources, it makes sense to do so prudently especially when agreeing to accept the services of someone who has a history of breaking the law.

If you have an especially discouraging job to do or one that requires a lot of lifting and moving that your usual volunteers can't or don't wish to handle, using court diversion could be a good solution and save your library some money. The task of cleaning out old storage rooms and moving the debris out for pick-up, for example, is not the kind of work you will typically find volunteers to do. In the end, many libraries end up hiring a local building company to come in or they use existing staff to get the job done. Rather than using precious staff time, or scarce financial resources, you might find this just the job for someone needing to do time for the community.

To find out more about the possibility of using court diversion, contact your local court system. Chances are that you will be able to get the help you need just for the asking. At the very least, you can register your interest and be put on the court's list as a potential placement site.

Advertising

If you have a special need for volunteers, either because of a special project coming up, or because you need to fill a special volunteer slot at the library, you may have the best luck if you advertise for exactly what you need. If you have a good relationship with the local newspaper, you may be able to convince them to put an ad in the paper for you as a gift to the library. If the need is truly great, you might ask the Friends to pay for an ad so you can get just the person or people you need.

Several years ago I worked for a library that was undergoing construction for a new addition. One of the major tasks involved in the project was the moving of the library's collection. We decided that we would get the job done by using a "human chain," taking books off the shelves in one area and handing them from person to person, shelving them in the new section. To make this chain work, we realized we would need approximately 100 people in the chain, with plenty of people in reserve filling in for those needing breaks.

In that small town, the idea of recruiting over 100 people to come in for three days seemed daunting. We decided that the best way to do it was to advertise. We placed advertisements in the local paper, with the local radio stations, and even in church bulletins. We explained what our plans were and what we needed volunteers to do. Volunteers were asked to call the library and sign up for a shift which might last anywhere from two hours to all day. The calls began to pour in. In fact, we received calls from people who didn't use the library but were interested in getting a chance to come inside and see how the construction was progressing.

To make the work more enjoyable, and to take care of volunteers who had agreed to stay all day, we solicited local restaurants to provide pizza, sandwiches and soft drinks for the volunteers. The event turned out to be so much fun (though tiring to be sure), many volunteers who had originally signed up for a short shift ended up staying all day. In addition, word of mouth brought in even more volunteers for the remaining two days of the project.

We may have been able to recruit volunteers for this project by appealing to the Friends, our regular patrons and our existing volunteers but by advertising, we were able to get the volunteers we needed with very little effort and in a very short time. At a time when our staff and volunteers were already overwhelmed by construction, simplicity and ease was greatly appreciated. The unexpected benefit was that we were able to include people who we didn't know and some who hadn't used the library in years in a fun community project.

Advertising might also be the best solution when you have need for a volunteer with very special talents. Some libraries, for example, have used volunteers to help index local newspapers or special collections. Volunteers have also been used when libraries opt to do retrospective conversion projects in-house. In these and similar cases, it makes sense to look for volunteers with excellent typing skills and some working knowledge of automated filing systems. In order to narrow the interest to those with the skills you need, advertising with skills required listed, will help you get the right people for the job.

If you decide that advertising makes sense for your particular volunteer needs, think about the requirements you need and be clear about them in the ad. Describe the volunteer opportunity clearly and present it in as positive light as possible to generate interest. It is probably possible to place the ad in a wide variety of places without spending much money—if you spend any money at all.

In addition to the local paper, place ads in your local "shopper's" newspaper, use public and community bulletin boards, post in-house flyers, place an ad in the Friends' newsletter, ask to post a notice at local schools where parents and students might see it, or place an ad in the high school or college paper. Another effective (and free!) strategy is to include special volunteer opportunities as a Public Service Announcement with your local radio stations. If you are really interested in targeting your search, consider approaching community organizations whose members are likely to have the skills you need and see if you can make an appeal through their own newsletter. If you have a landscape project, ask the garden club; if you want someone to set up a local magazine index and enter data, consult a local computer club.

One caveat: If you plan to put an ad in a local paper, do not ask for the volunteer ad to be placed in the "Help Wanted" section. People who are looking for jobs here are not likely to get excited about working for free! Instead, think about placing your ad in the "Personal" column and maybe even billing it as an opportunity to meet new people. See samples below and on page 37.

Meet new people. Broaden your horizons. Make a difference for our community. The Anycity Public Library is looking for a few special volunteers who will form a committee to conduct an inventory of the library's holdings. A general knowledge of libraries and of the Dewey Decimal system will be very helpful. Attention to detail and good follow-through are essential.

The entire project is expected to take approximately six months to complete but the hours are flexible. If you'd like the chance to try something new and work with others in the community to help the library, phone Jim at 123-4567.

Are you a person of creativity and vision? Do you have artistic talents or experience in graphic design? Do you have a background in marketing or retailing? Would you like the opportunity to work with other creative people in the community and display your talents citywide?

The Anycity Public Library is looking for a few special volunteers to work with the staff in designing and implementing a special promotional campaign to celebrate our new bookmobile service. We are interested in designing a comprehensive campaign that will take a multi-media approach to reach all members of our diverse community.

If you are interested in participating in this exciting project and can give an evening a week during the next two months to the library, please phone Jim at 123-4567.

Churches, Synagogues, Fellowships, etc.

Another good place to find people who are interested in doing community volunteer work is with the religious organizations in town. Many churches have special programs set up for the purpose of matching parishioners with volunteer opportunities within the city or town. Often, they are good places to look if you have a special project that requires the help of a lot of people for a short duration. Repainting the library's meeting room, moving books, setting up for the annual booksale are all times when local churches and synagogues can be contacted for help in recruiting volunteers.

A colleague of mine was pleasantly surprised when two members of the Church of the Latter Day Saints came into her library several years back to offer their volunteer services. These two young men told her that they were elders of the Church and as such had left their home in Salt Lake City to work and study in another community for two years. Part of their mission was to provide community service during their two-year study. They offered their services as a team and were willing to volunteer for four to six hours each week. As bright, dedicated and reliable young men, they ended up becoming invaluable volunteers.

Because of the requirements of their positions as elders, they brought their own cultural diversity into the library. Their religious mission meant that they were not allowed to do any reading with the exception of religious reading and that required for their volunteer positions. What seemed at first a fairly formal relationship between other staff members and the two elders became, in time, a very open and friendly relationship. In fact, because the situation worked out so well for everyone, these two young men recommended the library to new elders coming into the area and this library has had a steady stream of volunteer elders ever since.

My colleague has come to discover in talking with other librarians that such a situation is not unique. If your library does not currently enjoy the services of elders in your community, you might want to get in touch with your local Church of Latter Day Saints and discuss with them the possible placement of church members or elders wishing to provide community service.

Finding Volunteers to Work Off Premises

If you limit opportunities to on-site jobs only, you may be missing a willing and able pool of potential volunteers. There are probably many library jobs that can be done at home and there may well be people in your community who would love to work for you but who are homebound or institution-bound. Offering opportunities that could be done by someone who can't get to the library will broaden your volunteer pool significantly. Consider for example the possibility of assigning someone the responsibility of clipping and keeping a chronological file of all library related newspaper articles. A fairly competent person could also generate an index to those clippings giving your staff and your patrons an easy access to past library programs and events.

I know of one library that was able to use the special talents of a craftsperson in the community who could no longer walk and found it difficult to negotiate busy places with lots of activity even in a wheelchair. This woman was anxious to be able to make a meaningful contribution to the library which had begun delivering books to her at home. She suggested that the library think of some way of putting her handicraft talents and experience to work for them without requiring that she come to the library.

Without much hesitation, it was decided that this woman might be easily trained to mend books and so the most proficient book mender on staff took on the training of this special volunteer. In no time, the student had surpassed the instructor and I have found that to this day, this woman mends all library materials in need of repair and does so with perfection. Not only that, but the woman is so pleased at having meaningful and enjoyable work to do at home that she has been set up with supplies necessary for special materials in need of covering and once a week, both new materials that need special processing and older materials in need of repair are dropped off and completed work picked up. It's a very satisfactory arrangement for everyone.

Realizing that the talents, ability and sustained interest level will vary greatly among older people who reside in a community living situation, it still might be worthwhile to consider work that could be done by residents of adult day cares or continuing care facilities. Such simple projects as putting library event pictures and ephemera in albums or clipping library news could be completed by people who would enjoy and appreciate the opportunity to make a contribution even if they can't get to the library.

The Right Person for the Right Job

Ensuring that you give the volunteer the right job for him is critical to success. Because managing volunteers is more sensitive than managing paid staff, it can be extremely difficult to tell a volunteer that he is not performing up to your expectations and that you would like to move him to another position in the library. Sure, you can couch such lateral moves when they're necessary in terms of better utilizing his talent in another position, or by claiming a greater need in another area of service, but often a volunteer will see through such ruses. It is always much better to avoid such an unpleasant task from the beginning if at all possible.

The best opportunity you'll probably ever have for ensuring that you give a volunteer a job where he can succeed, is at the very beginning of his volunteer employment. All the careful steps you take before you hire someone should be taken for the volunteer as well. In fact, because realistically you do not have the option of progressive discipline to deal with poor performance from a volunteer, it is critical that you take advantage of the best chance you have to put a volunteer exactly where you want him—where his talents will serve you best or where he can make a positive contribution despite a possible lack of useful skills or talent. That chance is at the start of his employment.

The Application Process

Beginning with the application process and following through with an extensive interview that includes a check of his references, you can get much of the information you need to make a wise decision regarding the placement of a new volunteer. Many libraries use some form of volunteer application form even if they are bringing someone on board that was specially recruited. Such a form will allow you to find out about a volunteer's talents and interests and past experience. It should include a space for current references that you are sure to check! (See sample Volunteer Application Form, page 41.)

Once a potential volunteer has filled out an application form, he should be invited in for an interview. This is an important time in the application process because this will be your chance to develop a sense of the potential volunteer's strengths and weaknesses and it will give you a chance to talk about possible volunteer openings.

Unless a volunteer has been specially recruited for his special talents or to fill a temporary need, it makes sense to begin volunteers at the lowest task level possible commensurate with his skills, abilities, or special talents. Even a volunteer with outstanding experience and credentials can surprise you, and if you've placed him in a volunteer position that requires more skill and talent than other more routine jobs, you will find yourself in the uncomfortable position of moving him down in the ranks. And don't kid yourself that moves within the library will be seen as lateral. If you've hired a seemingly friendly person with a strong public relations background to work at the welcome desk and find him to be gruff and terse, you won't be fooling him if you ask a week later that he read shelves instead. Best to hire volunteers for the simple, back room tasks first, then move them up to more public and/or complex tasks if your good instincts about them pan out.

During the interview process, it is likely that a potential volunteer will be very forceful about what he would like his job in

VOLUNTEER APPLICATION FORM

NOTICE TO APPLICANT: Thank you for your interest in serving our community through work at the Anycity Public Library. Volunteers are a very important component of our workforce. Because we rely on our volunteers to enable us to provide the best service possible to the community, we ask that they commit to an agreed upon schedule and give reasonable notice if they are unable to report to work. Excessive absences make it difficult for us to work efficiently. If a volunteer finds that he or she must miss work frequently, the library may find it necessary to replace him or her with someone who is able to be on hand on a regular basis.

Volunteers are required to attend special staff meetings one to three times per year. Each volunteer will be evaluated individually on a formal basis once a year and informally throughout the year.

The volunteer coordinator will determine the nature and scope of each volunteer's job in the library within two weeks of the initial interview.

NAME _____

PHONE _____

ADDRESS _____

CONTACT PERSON (in case of emergency) _____
_____ PHONE _____

1. List past work experience (including volunteer work). Highlight the experience which you feel might be applicable to library work.

2. List other skills and special knowledge you have which might be beneficial to the library.

3. Why are you interested in Anycity Public Library?

4. Are you interested in all aspects of library work? Are there some jobs you are not interested in?

5. Would you prefer to have a regular work schedule or work on special projects within a more flexible time frame?

6. Are there any days or times of day when you are not available?

7. Are there any days or times of day when you would prefer to work?

8. How many hours per week/month would you have to give to the library?

REFERENCES:

1. _____

    PHONE _____

2. _____

    PHONE _____

_____

Applicant signature

_____

Date

the library to be. Again, it makes sense to place the volunteer in a lower level position to begin with. Even if you believe that this person would be suited to the volunteer work he is interested in, if it's work that needs a special kind of person, hold back until you have a chance to evaluate him in the work place. While it's true that you could lose a potentially valuable volunteer by screening in this manner, you gain in the long run by giving yourself the opportunity to evaluate performance and reward volunteers by moving them "up the ladder."

Because volunteers have wide ranging skills and abilities, you shouldn't assume that any volunteer can handle any simple task. Shelving books may seem easy to you, but there are many people, for example, who just can't make sense of the dewey decimal system — why doesn't 17 come *after* 2 as in 917.17 v. 917.2 — after all 17 is larger than 2!

Believe it or not, I know of a library who unwittingly hired a volunteer who couldn't read and then set this volunteer to the task of filing! The sad reality was that rather than admit she couldn't read, this volunteer spent long hours painstakingly matching letter against letter before it was discovered that the inordinate amount of time it was taking her to complete the task was due to an inability to read.

Certainly there were other jobs in the library that this volunteer could have managed well such as taking care of the library's plants or dusting shelves, or putting mylar jackets on books. Instead, the situation became an embarrassment for everyone and was resolved only when the volunteer quit in frustration. It's fairly easy to avoid the potential of giving a volunteer a task he is incapable of handling. If you will be requiring a volunteer to file, shelve books, or engage in any other kind of clerical work, you might administer a very simple clerical test that you have designed to determine a potential volunteer's aptitude for a particular task. It shouldn't be a complicated or intimidating test — certainly no more than 20 questions. (See example on page 44.)

Once the interview is over, you still have one more step to follow before assigning a job. You still need to check the volunteer's references. Making good placement decisions for volunteers is extremely important — as important as hiring any employee. Remember, the best chance you have of getting the right volunteer for the right job is at the very beginning of the application process and an important component of that process is checking references.

I heard the story of one volunteer coordinator who was initially delighted to receive the services of a young woman who came to her and said that she would be happy to volunteer her time and talent for data entry if the library had any use for such services. This volunteer, "Betsy," said she was a fast and accurate typist, and that she actually enjoyed the work of data entry; she said that she found it relaxing. Because the library was in the process of automating and

LIBRARY SKILLS AND APTITUDE MEASUREMENT

1. Please put the following titles in alphabetical order (1–5)
   with #1 being the first title alphabetically:

   _____ *A Yellow Raft in Blue Water*
   _____ *Yell Down the Water Spout*
   _____ *Yesterday's Gone*
   _____ *Yeoman from Madrid*
   _____ *Yellowing Dreams*

2. Please put the following numbers in correct order (1–5)
   with #1 being the lowest number and #5 the highest:

   _____ 917.17
   _____ 917.22
   _____ 920.09
   _____ 917.4
   _____ 920

3. Please put the following author names in alphabetical order
   (1–5) with #1 being the first author alphabetically:

   _____ Smith, John C.
   _____ Smiley, Jane
   _____ Thompson, Richard
   _____ Thompsen, Thomas
   _____ Smith, John Witherall

was getting ready to create a patron database, Betsy, who was willing to work several mornings a week, seemed heaven sent.

Sure enough, Betsy was fast and accurate. She was also very foul-mouthed and talked to herself and the computer almost constantly. Upon hearing a barrage of complaints from Betsy's fellow workers, the volunteer coordinator isolated Betsy claiming a need of space and the desire to give Betsy a quiet space where she could concentrate on her work. Not content to converse solely with her computer, however, Betsy found her way back into the workroom often during her shift, interrupting other workers, complaining about glitches or minor problems and bringing her foul mouth with her.

Since a simple solution of isolation didn't work, the volunteer coordinator spoke frankly with Betsy, telling her that others found her language offensive and that if at all possible, she should direct her questions and concerns only to her as volunteer coordinator. This necessary and frank discussion was met with an out-and-out tirade. The volunteer coordinator reported that Betsy screamed at her, and even threatened to erase the work she'd done to date. Then she stomped out of the building—happily, never to be seen again.

Going back over Betsy's application form to look for something that might have predicted such a problem, the volunteer coordinator saw that Betsy had listed a neighboring library as a reference. In calling this library to see what their experience with Betsy had been, the volunteer coordinator found that they had experienced Betsy's foul mouth and moodiness, too, but had "quickly run out of work for Betsy to do" so were able to get rid of her without the ugly scene.

The moral of the story is obvious. You wouldn't hire a staff member without checking references, so don't hire a volunteer without doing the same. Even if you believe in offering everyone a chance, you might legitimately question that belief when it comes to knowingly accepting someone who at worst is mentally unbalanced and at best cannot function in the library's social environment.

It makes sense to have a consistent procedure on what action will be taken at the conclusion of the interview. If your library is small and your volunteer force quite manageable, you may make it a matter of policy to offer a position at the conclusion of the interview—this makes sense especially if you have recruited or interviewed a potential volunteer for a specific job but it does eliminate your ability to call references and make a deliberate decision on where this volunteer will fit in best.

Most libraries would do well to make it a policy to get back to a potential volunteer within a certain specified time frame. This option allows you to think about the applicant in terms of the various opportunities you have available. If you have any concerns or questions about a potential volunteer, a waiting period gives you some time to call references. In addition, if the volunteer is to be successful in his new job, he will need good training. Who will be doing the training? Who will be the new volunteer's mentor? Mandating a waiting period will give you an opportunity to schedule the necessary training and to ensure that the new volunteer will be placed where he is needed most and can do the best job.

Whatever decision you make regarding a waiting period before offering a position, be absolutely sure that the applicant knows when he will be contacted regarding a job and then, *contact him when promised.* No matter how busy you are, it is essential that you get back to potential volunteers when you have promised to do so. Nothing will harm the library's good reputation as a volunteer site than the lack of simple courtesy to those who are offering you their time and talent. If you are unable to make a decision within the promised time-frame, a postcard letting the potential volunteer know that you are thinking of him but have not had the opportunity to set up the training required will be welcomed. And again, give the potential volunteer a new time-frame when he can expect to hear from you.

If you are unable to find the time to get back to potential volunteers within a reasonable period of time, you probably are not ready to set up and maintain a viable volunteer workforce. If this is the case, use the missed opportunities (i.e., those who have come to you offering their help) as ammunition to get the additional staffing required to manage volunteers. Letting your funding authorities know that you are foregoing *free help* for lack of adequate staffing to recruit, manage and train volunteers can be a powerful tool to get the funding you need.

In the meantime, be sure that you are able to provide both existing volunteers and potential volunteers with the support they need and deserve. Potential volunteers should be contacted when promised then, if hired, trained and supervised so that they can be true assets to the library's operations.

Whom Should You Hire as a Volunteer?

The simple answer to this question is: anyone who wants to give time to the library. With few exceptions, as with the case of Betsy above, almost anyone who wants to give time to the library has something of value to contribute. No matter how limited a person's abilities and talents are, there is almost always something he can do that will make a meaningful difference. Tasks as simple but important as collecting materials left around the reading room and returning them to circulation for re-shelving, pasting in book pockets, stamping of date due cards, picking up the library's lawn and keeping it free of debris, covering books; as well as more complex tasks such as indexing special collections, updating patron files, developing special mailing lists, etc. are all important and all contribute to our ability to deliver quality service.

You will enhance your library's public image tremendously if you back up the concept that it is, indeed, the *public's* library by allowing the public to participate in the delivery of service. Not only do you create a sense of pride and ownership within your community by nurturing an active volunteer force, you enable your staff to be more productive, you can increase the diversity of the workforce, and you can even create a strong political base of support among your volunteers.

Remember, those who volunteer their services to the library often have the most compelling voices in the community. When volunteers speak out on the library's behalf, they are not only viewed as having a lack of any self-interest, they also have the added impact of having put their money (in this case their time) where their mouths are. Volunteers can be your best goodwill ambassadors. They represent all segments of the community and they will spread the good word about library services better than almost anyone else can.

3

Training, Development, and Evaluation

Training

The success of each volunteer to make a meaningful contribution to the library and to truly enjoy the experience will depend upon her being placed appropriately and then well trained for the position, as well as being thoroughly integrated into the social and professional fabric of the library. We all know how important training is for new staff members; it provides the foundation upon which future performance will be built. In the case of volunteers, a good foundation is, perhaps, even more critical.

Many new volunteers come to you without prior library experience. In some cases, new volunteers come without solid work skills or they come with skills that they haven't used for a number of years. Add to this the fact that many volunteers will only be working for you for a few hours a week, eliminating the day to day learning and experience that establishes consistency and confidence in handling even routine tasks. Without this daily experience and exposure to their work, deviations in the quality of their performance can be especially difficult to handle in a successful way.

The best chance you will have to ensure that a volunteer's performance and contribution are the best they can be is to provide good, solid training up front and to provide continuous evaluation and support throughout their employ. While it is true that training, especially good thorough training, takes precious staff time—time that, initially at least, is not compensated by the volunteer's assistance—it is also true that the better the training the better the performance. The better the performance, the happier and more fulfilled the volunteer will feel in her position. Happy and fulfilled employees, whether paid or volunteer, deliver their best. It's a circular scenario of the very best kind.

Beginning with Day One

For many people, entering a new work environment for the first time can be a little scary. A new volunteer is not likely to know her fellow workers and may not be sure exactly what her job will entail or how well she'll be able to do it. Even if the job itself is clear enough, she may not be certain exactly what your expectations for performance are. All these are elements that can cause some unease in the beginning but are easily resolved, and it's up to the volunteer supervisor to resolve them.

Because any work site with two or more people has a social element to it, it makes sense to ensure that a new person coming into that environment feels comfortable on a social level. Providing a new volunteer with a mentor is an excellent way to introduce her to the library, its social structure and its working environment. A mentor can fill a volunteer in on the more human side of the library, explaining the administrative hierarchy and sharing information about the corporate culture—those values and service philosophies of the library that may be unwritten.

While the mentor may not be the person doing the actual job training for the volunteer, it makes sense to provide for the new volunteer a person they feel comfortable asking questions of, and a person who will introduce them to their future co-workers. If the first shift of a new volunteer is a short one, it may best be spent in getting a "back stage" tour of the library followed by an informal discussion of library philosophy. This is the perfect chance for the new volunteer to ask questions about the library and most importantly, to get a clear understanding of just how her work will contribute to library service as a whole.

The most important thing you can do on a volunteer's first day is make the workplace welcoming. For many volunteers, this volunteer job may be the first work experience since retirement—certainly for most it will be the first work experience at *this* library.

The first day can be overwhelming and unsettling. You can increase the comfort level for a new volunteer by ensuring that she is made to feel as welcomed as she truly is and to see to it that she isn't hit with too many job requirements and tasks right away. By taking it slow and easy, and by helping the volunteer feel part of the team, you will likely increase the volunteer's enthusiasm for and commitment to the library.

After the new volunteer has been taken around and introduced, after getting a tour of the library along with a discussion of how different library departments work together to provide service, the volunteer can be taken to her own work site and shown how she will perform her job. At this point, a new volunteer may be introduced to the person who will handle the actual training—mentor and trainer need not necessarily be the same person. In fact, if the mentor is not responsible for training, you will have provided the volunteer with two contacts she feels comfortable with before the end of the first day!

Putting It in Writing

Once you have established a comfortable social introduction to the library for the new volunteer, it's time to respond to another important element in training that will help ensure success: the library's expectations for performance. Every library department should have a procedures manual to help train new employees and volunteers, and to help refresh the memories of staff members who must occasionally face situations that come up too seldom to be remembered. Although procedures manuals can be a bit overwhelming to new employees and volunteers who are sure they will *never* remember all the information, they do provide written underpinning of what you will be teaching and in the end, that should provide some comfort or at least some answers to the many questions about her job that the volunteer is likely to have at first.

Depending on your library, the number of positions you have for both paid employees and for volunteers, your procedures manuals could be anything from a 100+ page document, to a few pages of instructions, stapled together and photocopied for each member of the entire crew. Whatever the sophistication, it will improve training (and the on-going quality of your staff's work) to provide some written instruction on how particular jobs are to be done.

There is a right way and a wrong way to do everything, from answering the phone and routing the calls, to covering books, to working on a special project to enhance visibility for the library. Don't make the volunteer guess or increase the opportunity for the volunteer to forget an important instruction and make a mistake. Take time in the very beginning, on the very first day, to provide the volunteer with some written guidelines about your expectations for performance in the particular volunteer job you have assigned as well as your expectations for all library staff members — volunteer or not.

Even better than giving a new volunteer the staff procedures manual is to provide volunteers with a special procedures manual designed specifically for volunteers — and perhaps even designed for specific volunteer jobs. Designing and updating such a manual need not be overwhelming especially if experienced volunteers play a major role in its development! If wordprocessing is used and the manual saved on disk, it can be easily modified as necessary.

Be sure to set an upbeat tone in the beginning by letting volunteers know how important they are to the success of the library. Begin your manual (or written instructions) with your library's mission statement and include a philosophy statement about the importance of libraries, the importance of library personnel, and the very special importance of volunteers.

In addition to making a general statement about the importance of volunteer contribution to library services, be specific. How many volunteers served the library in the preceding year? What kinds of jobs have volunteers done? In what specific ways have volunteers made a difference for the library and the community it serves? It's so important to let volunteers know right up front that you value them and the contributions they make. Remember, volunteers will be giving you so much more than their time. They will be giving you their moral and political support — if they feel they are valued, that is; if they do not ever get the sense that they are being taken for granted.

After stating the value of volunteers to the library in general and specific terms, state what exactly the volunteer job consists of and how it should be done. There should be a written job description available for each volunteer position in the library. If you do not currently have such job descriptions in place, creating them need not be a daunting task—even if you have a volunteer force numbering in the hundreds! Regardless of the number of volunteers you have, the number of unique positions is probably far lower than the number of actual volunteers. Furthermore, volunteer job descriptions need not be elaborate. One page is probably all you need to describe any particular job. (See sample volunteer job descriptions, pages 54–56.)

If you are in the position of recruiting a volunteer for a new position or special project, put your needs for the position or project in writing. Not only will this help clarify your search and enable you to get the right person for the right job, it will provide the framework (if not the actual article) for that particular volunteer job description.

Progressive Training

Even in the simplest of volunteer jobs, there are bound to be a few complexities—a few exceptions to the rules. However well trained you feel a volunteer to be after her first day, don't abandon the role of training just yet. It will be important for both the volunteer's confidence and the future sustained quality of the volunteer's performance, that you spend a good amount of time with her during her second shift and perhaps even her third and fourth with a gradual reduction in direct oversight and supervision. Even for the simplest of jobs, it's important for you to reinforce the importance of the job, the importance of its being done correctly and consistently, and to answer any questions the new volunteer has about the job or the library as she begins to learn the ropes.

For the more complex volunteer jobs, continued one-on-one training is especially important. Again, the investment you are willing to make at this important initial juncture will pay you back many times over with a volunteer who knows her job well and whose work can be counted on to be self-directed and of high quality. Because it is often the case that volunteers come to you without library experience, it's very important not to take things too fast. Some elements of the job that seem self-evident to you will be mysterious to someone who has never worked in a library before. Also, be sure to avoid library jargon. To us "circulation" describes the

SAMPLE VOLUNTEER JOB DESCRIPTION #1

LIBRARY HOST

The Library Host is an important and visible position. The Host is the first person our patrons see when they enter the building. The job of the Host is to welcome patrons, create a cheerful atmosphere, and direct patrons with particular requests to the appropriate department.

The Library Host gives information to new patrons about the library, its services, and how community members can obtain a library card.

Specific Duties and Responsibilities

- Greets patrons entering the library.
- Is fully informed about what services the library offers the community and our patrons.
- Understands the policy regarding library cards and is able to explain to new patrons how to obtain one.
- Directs patrons to appropriate departments based on their particular needs. For example, sends those wishing to sign up for storytime to the Children's Room, those with reference questions to the reference desk, those with questions about overdue materials to the circulation desk.
- Provides interested patrons with current library promotional materials such as flyers advertising upcoming programs, the library's newsletter, and the library's welcome brochure.

Position Requirements

A cheerful demeanor, good oral communication skills, and a genuine desire to serve the public. Thorough knowledge of building geography and staff persons on duty is required.

LIBRARY MATERIALS PROCESSOR

The Library Materials Processor covers and prepares library materials to make them more attractive and to increase their durability before they are made available to the public.

Duties and Responsibilities

- Covers books, both hard cover and paperback in accordance with established library procedure (see individual instruction sheets for various types of library materials).

- Processes videos, cassettes, CDs, and other library media in accordance with established library procedure (see individual instruction sheets for library media).

- Follows inventory procedures for processing supplies and notifies supervisor when replacements need to be ordered.

- Repairs and replaces worn or damaged book covers as necessary and informs supervisor when repair or replacement of covers is not possible or attractive.

- Recommends new procedures or supplies that might make the processing of materials easier, less expensive, more enduring, or more attractive.

Position Requirements

This position requires good handiwork skills, along with neatness and attention to detail. The person in this position should be able to follow simple inventory procedures and be able to judge when the repair or replacement of book and media covers will not make the material suitable for patron use.

SAMPLE VOLUNTEER JOB DESCRIPTION #3

SHELVER

Accurate shelving is one of the most important jobs in the library. Shelvers must be committed to paying close attention to detail to ensure that every book is returned to its appropriate place on the shelf. The Anycity Public Library has over 75,000 volumes. If a book is shelved in the wrong place, it may never be found by patrons looking for it. Misshelved books are often assumed to be "missing" and are replaced, costing the library hundreds of dollars a year and keeping important resources out of the hands of those who need them.

Duties and Responsibilities

- Has thorough knowledge and understanding of the filing rules for the Dewey Decimal System.
- Ensures that each book has been appropriately checked in according to the procedures in the "Circulation Procedures Manual."
- Accurately shelves books and other library materials in their appropriate position.
- Checks surrounding area while shelving on a continuous basis to identify areas where library materials have been misshelved.
- Reshelves appropriately, any books or other library material found to have been misshelved.
- Re-sets loose book-ends, straightens books that have slipped, keeps shelves looking neat and tidy.

Position Requirements

This position requires great attention to detail and a willingness to interrupt his/her own work to correct the misshelving of others. An understanding and respect for the importance of accurate and neat shelving is essential.

process of checking materials in and out. To almost everyone else, "circulation" describes what's happening to the blood in our bodies!

The best training method I know of for more complex jobs is one where the job is broken down into its various elements and taught one element at a time. As a volunteer becomes extremely familiar with one aspect of the job, she can build on it with the next component. It takes patience, sometimes for both the volunteer and supervisor, not to rush on too soon with the training. Remember, volunteers often work only once a week (sometimes less) for typically short periods of time.

A volunteer is much more likely to remember from shift to shift, one simple element of a job that she repeated over and over on the first shift than a set of complex instructions. It is much better to build on a solid and simple foundation than to continually repeat all the elements of a job that were given at once on the first day and subsequently forgotten or half-remembered.

On-Going Reinforcement

Even the best volunteers need training reinforcement from time to time just as your paid employees do. Jobs change, policies change, and even the environment in which a job is performed changes. All these factors can and do impact a volunteer's performance level and comfort with her job.

Technology, for example, can alter the way in which a volunteer does her job, and if technology has caused a change, it's important that the volunteer get more than just a cursory explanation of how to modify her work. Just as you respect and accommodate a volunteer's inexperience when she begins her position at the library, you should respect that same inexperience which may make accommodation to technological changes especially difficult.

When changes in routine occur, use the same training techniques you used when the volunteer first started. First, explain carefully what the change will be and why it's needed. Then let the volunteer know how important her role in the change will be and how much you value her contribution—especially now in a changing environment. Finally, break down the necessary changes into their simplest components and carefully teach these new components one at a time until the volunteer can perform as well as at previous levels.

Sometimes a change in library policy will force a change in a volunteer's workload or in the very way in which she does her job. Sometimes these policy changes will completely eliminate one component of a job while introducing a new one. Suppose, for example, that you have a volunteer helping you process library materials before they are put in circulation. The volunteer covers books, and prepares audio-visual materials. A decision by the library to add music CDs and computer software to the circulating collection while eliminating music cassettes will have an obvious impact on this volunteer's job. Furthermore, it may be the decision of library management to push the music CDs for awhile to introduce this new material to the public.

Such decisions can mean more than just the development of new skills, it may also mean a change in work flow—even if temporary. It's important to let the volunteer know that CDs will take precedence in the processing order and it is also important to explain why. Volunteers have opinions, too! Policy and procedure changes are likely to be approved or disapproved of by volunteer staff members, even if they never say a word. If a volunteer who came to process library materials because she believes so much in the importance of reading gets the idea that books don't matter anymore to the administration, her own morale can decline and she is likely to be a far less favorable advocate of the library's when she discusses new policy with her friends and neighbors outside the library. It's both respectful and smart to let a volunteer know *why* changes are being made as well as *how* they will change her job.

Even if a volunteer's job remains the same over time, the work environment is likely to change. In fact, in most libraries, the work environment has changed dramatically during recent years. For one thing, most libraries are finding that use is increasing yearly while budgets remain stagnant, or worse yet, have declined (that's why volunteers have become more important!). What this means, of course, is that we are all working harder to deliver services, and the level of stress in the work environment increases.

In-house workshops are often used successfully to train workers how to manage and increase workflow, how to reduce stress in the workplace and how to communicate effectively with co-workers. These workshops might not relieve extremely busy situations or totally eliminate stress but they will teach ways to cope more effectively with a busy and sometimes stressful environment. As the use of the library grows, both staff and volunteers should be given periodic instruction on how best to handle the changing conditions in their workplace that such growth causes.

Add to heavier work loads the fact that libraries are seeing more homeless and displaced persons in libraries than ever before. Volunteers who work in public areas of the library are likely to encounter patrons who do not fit with their idea of the "traditional" patron and that can make them feel uncomfortable. In these cases, it's very important that volunteers understand the library's policies with regard to service for all people regardless of circumstance, lifestyle or background.

If your library is seeing more and more "non-traditional" patrons, it is likely that your paid staff, too, is feeling uncomfortable and maybe even at risk. In this case, it makes sense to bring in outside experts to talk to both staff and volunteers about dealing effectively with different and diverse patrons and how to identify someone who may need help or who may actually pose a safety risk.

More and more libraries are offering staff "gatekeeper" training to help identify members of the public who might be in need of social or medical assistance. If your library is offering such training, be sure to include those volunteers who are also serving the public.

It's vitally important to a confident and productive volunteer workforce that you don't drop the ball on training once you feel the volunteer is proficient in her job. Most jobs change over time and often ways of doing things must be modified or changed altogether. In addition, changes in the library itself can make volunteers less effective or less comfortable with their jobs. It makes sense to keep the lines of communication open, especially with regard to needs for additional training or job support.

When Training Doesn't Work

Once in awhile, even the most diligent and careful training won't be enough to gradually turn the reigns of a job over to the volunteer you've selected to fill it. For whatever reason, there are times when a volunteer who seems to be perfectly capable just doesn't get it. Even after breaking the components of a job down is its most simple elements and going over them in a patient and consistent way, some volunteers just can't seem to put the entire job together.

After a while, you realize that your time as a supervisor is under constant demand from a volunteer who forgets how to do a particular aspect of her job, who is intimidated or confused by even minor variances in the workflow, or who just plain lacks the confidence or skill to be left alone to perform the job.

When you feel that adequate training time has passed and you are convinced that you've done everything possible to assure good training and the volunteer is still dependent on an inordinate amount of assistance either by the supervisor or by her co-workers, it makes sense to re-evaluate the situation and your placement of the volunteer. Before approaching the volunteer with your concerns, consider carefully the aspects of the job that give this volunteer the most trouble. Think about alternative volunteer jobs that wouldn't require the skills that the volunteer has been unable to master in this particular position.

Once you feel you've identified the problem and have come up with an alternative job in the library that the volunteer could probably handle more easily, it is time to talk to the volunteer. As tough as it may feel, the old adage is very true here: honesty is the best policy. Let the volunteer know that given the amount of time and training you have allotted, you feel the volunteer should have mastered the job by now. Admit that the job match wasn't a good one and that that was your fault. Let the volunteer know that in the course of management, change is often necessary to ensure that the right person has the right job. Let the volunteer see through your eyes. What areas have you observed giving her trouble? She doesn't work well alone, for example, or she has a hard time with fine motor skills if she's processing materials.

If you've been practicing good training techniques, you should not be met with any surprises. This is not the time, for example, to find out that the equipment offered the volunteer to do the job is inadequate or that the volunteer isn't getting the job done because of constant interruptions. All these sorts of "fixable" difficulties that can arise for a new volunteer, should have been noted and addressed as they first became known—during the training process.

In actuality, once you've gone through the training process and have given the volunteer plenty of time to learn, she will know as well as you that it's not working if it isn't. It may be a bit of a blow to the ego when you finally point this out, but it will probably be a relief as well. Be prepared with another job offer at which this volunteer should be more successful. Present the job change in a positive light and let the volunteer know that this alternative job is equally important and you feel more well suited to this volunteer's abilities.

There are times, of course, when you meet up with a volunteer who can't seem to function well and/or independently in *any* position and such cases can be very difficult. Some volunteers are indeed "challenging" (see Chapter 4), but given some creative thinking and patience, it's surprising how often a satisfactory solution can be found for both the library and the volunteer.

Development

Special Opportunities for Volunteer Development

If in-house training workshops are important ways to reinforce training and help volunteers do their jobs more effectively, educational opportunities outside the library can be equally effective if not more so. It's easy for any of us to become fairly insular in our thinking and set in our ways. Training sessions that are provided by non-library personnel who are experts in the fields of time management, stress relief, communication techniques, customer relations, team building, and organizational planning often bring with them fresh perspectives and new ideas.

It is likely that your library is already taking advantage of opportunities in the community, region or state to enhance staff development and performance. But does your library utilize some of these same continuing education opportunities for your volunteer workforce? If not, maybe you should consider it. Volunteers have as much to gain as staff members — in fact, they may have more to gain. Volunteers who, typically, do not work as many hours a week as most staff members and who often work more irregularly, are quite likely to be in need of additional reinforcement of public service and work skills.

By sending volunteers out to such workshops and training sessions, you not only increase their value to your library, you also send an important message to the volunteer—a message that says, "you matter to us and we value your professional growth as we do all our employees." Such training is often free or of minimal expense, and what you gain is a volunteer with a deeper understanding of a particular aspect of her job and most likely, one who is now even more loyal to the library.

In addition to non-library opportunities, there are opportunities throughout the year to increase a volunteer's level of performance in a directly related way. Regional and state library conferences and workshops are excellent opportunities to enable your volunteers to learn more about libraries in general and more about library issues and practices in particular. Those of us who regularly attend such conferences and workshops already know that they can be enlightening and rejuvenating. Certainly volunteers deserve the same chance to learn, to meet others in the library world, and to come back to their positions refreshed, better informed, and perhaps more confident and proud in their role at the library.

There's an added benefit, too, in encouraging volunteers to become more active in library association functions. The more deeply they become involved in libraries, the more likely they are to be active and vocal spokespeople for libraries. It will certainly be easier to get a volunteer's assistance in generating community support for the library if she has learned both in the library and outside of it how important libraries are in society and is able to articulate that importance on your behalf.

The Volunteer Supervisor

Supervising volunteers can be a very challenging and time consuming job. Some larger libraries, and those that use volunteers quite extensively, have a person on staff whose sole responsibility is to recruit, hire, place, train and evaluate volunteers. There are even libraries who fill the position of volunteer supervisor with a full-time volunteer! Of course, if you are using a volunteer as a volunteer supervisor, or even thinking about it, you might consider the long-term implications of such a move. For one thing, the more successful your volunteer program (and a special volunteer supervisor is likely to increase your chances of success), the more the program will grow and become more and more demanding for the supervisor.

As discussed in Chapter 1, it doesn't make sense in the long run to use volunteers for a permanent position that requires special skills not easily replaced with another "generic" volunteer. Certainly, the management of volunteers in any library requires a great deal of skill and some very special talent. A successful volunteer program is such a valuable asset for any library, that to risk its future health on your questionable ability to find a "free" replacement if your unpaid volunteer supervisor leaves may be unwise. Furthermore, if your volunteer force is at all sizable and is growing or you wish to expand it, you probably want the person in charge of its welfare fully accountable and that is usually done best with a paycheck!

If you've concluded that you don't want to place the responsibility for your volunteer workforce in the hands of a volunteer, then there are several other options that have worked well for many libraries which are tailored to each library's unique staffing situations and volunteer workforce. If your volunteer staff is somewhat small in relation to paid staff and is fairly stable in terms of growth, it may be that one member of the staff can have included in her duties the oversight for volunteer management. This person may be responsible for recruiting volunteers as needed, fielding applications from people who simply show up and offer their services, interviewing and placing volunteers, and assisting with their annual evaluation and with recognition and appreciation events.

The beauty of this plan is that one single person has oversight of the volunteer situation in the library. Your volunteer coordinator knows what departments in the library have volunteer jobs available, which existing volunteers can be counted on to take on extra responsibilities from time to time or could easily be reassigned according to need, as well as which volunteers are struggling and perhaps need reassignment or reinforcement. With one special person in charge of volunteer management, the approach the library is able to take with recruitment, training, and evaluation is consistent and likely to evolve into a better program because one person is learning from mistakes as well as from experiments and approaches that work.

Furthermore, with one person ultimately in charge of volunteers, you are more likely to have uniform volunteer assistance throughout the library. A single volunteer coordinator will be aware of all the gaps and will be working to fill them on an equitable basis. In the end, one person is accountable for the volunteer program in the library, and that makes things very simple from a management perspective.

The obvious drawback of designating one person on staff as the volunteer manager is time. Is there someone on your staff who is available to take on this extra work—work that is likely to grow if this staff member is good at it? If not, do you have money in the budget to hire someone especially for the job? Even if you imagine this position to be part-time, it is getting increasingly difficult for many libraries to convince policy makers to authorize money for additional staff.

In the case of a volunteer supervisor, however, you may be able to make a strong case to even the toughest of city managers or town councils. It might be easier than you think to convince your funders that a volunteer manager will pay for herself if she's able to develop a viable and strong volunteer force. Just be careful if you take this approach that you don't oversell the idea of volunteers. It's hard enough to convince government leaders that running a library is a complex task that requires many levels of skills and education. Too many government leaders lacking an appreciation for what we do will be only too delighted to do what they might believe is supporting a conversion of paid employees to a volunteer workforce. In selling such a position, be sure that you are careful to explain that a good volunteer workforce *assists* the staff in the accomplishment of their duties; that a good volunteer workforce enables the staff to be more productive—they do not eliminate the need for staff.

I know of a library that had to face a real threat in a small New England town by a Selectboard that was convinced money could be saved if library staff could be at least partially eliminated with a concerted effort to beef up the volunteer staff. Ironically, what precipitated the debate was a report made by the library director touting the number of volunteer hours donated to the library in the annual report. What made the threat truly serious was the recommendation of the Selectboard that a hiring freeze be instituted and left in place for two years in order to determine exactly what roles volunteers could play in the maintenance of library services.

Happily, it was the volunteer force at this library that came to the rescue. When informed of the very real possibility that positions would remain open as an "experiment" to see just how far a volunteer workforce could go, the volunteers panicked! Luckily in most of New England, the town meeting still offers the opportunity for community input prior to the ratification of a budget. At the town meeting, library volunteers turned up in force. "Do you have any idea what it takes to run a library?" they asked the Selectboard. They explained, fairly passionately, that they lacked the skills, time and even the inclination to provide what was necessary to deliver comprehensive service. "Don't put this responsibility on us," they explained, "we're not capable of meeting it and we don't want it." Thanks to these volunteers, the idea was put quickly to rest when it became obvious that it was ill-conceived and didn't even consider the willingness or talents of the very people it would have utilized to replace paid library positions.

For many libraries, the idea of a single person in sole charge of the volunteer workforce is only fantasy. No one on staff has an extra minute in her day to take on the responsibility and no amount of negotiation has brought in the revenue needed to create a new position — even if only part-time. In cases like this, each department head or coordinator works independently to fill the volunteer needs in her own department. Recruiting may be on-going by various departments in the library and each department takes on the orientation, training, and evaluation separately.

While such a fragmented approach may honestly be the only one available for understaffed libraries, it certainly has its drawbacks. First of all, unless communication among departments is excellent, there are likely to be inconsistencies in the expectations that are set for performance, the methods used for evaluation and recognition, and in the way volunteers who don't meet expectations are handled. All of this can cause some morale problems among volunteers and certainly decrease the effectiveness of volunteers from one department to another.

If it is necessary for your library to leave volunteer management in the hands of department coordinators, it is very important that as a group, department coordinators or department heads work out a set of standards for recruiting, placing, training and evaluating volunteers. In addition, it makes sense to do some cooperative "cross training" of volunteers for various departments so that if a volunteer is working in one department, she can be easily shifted to work in another. This also makes sense from an economic perspective. The more well rounded any volunteer is in terms of training, the more valuable she is to your organization as a whole.

Another possibility, especially for smaller libraries, is to put the responsibility for volunteer management in the hands of the director or assistant director. These people are busy too, of course, but they have the advantage of having a more global perspective of library operations. The director or assistant director will know where the gaps are in the library with regard to volunteer staffing and be in a good position to help fill them in a uniform way helping to ensure that there is a balance in volunteer services provided and that they are provided where needed most.

Whoever ends up in charge of volunteer management at your library, it is important to recognize that this role is an important and sometimes difficult one. Just as volunteers need training and reinforcement, so does the volunteer supervisor. Luckily, in even the smallest of communities there are often support groups and training sessions for supervisors of volunteers.

Because most nonprofit agencies depend upon volunteers for the delivery of service, these agencies are employing or assigning the role of volunteer supervisor just as you are. If you do not receive information about workshops and training sessions developed for these supervisors, contact your local hospital, Retired Seniors Volunteer Program (RSVP), or even your local chamber of commerce to find out if such programs are available from time to time in your community. Very often these workshops are held locally, are very inexpensive, and can provide valuable support and insight to help those managing volunteers.

If you are unable to find programs or workshops in or near your community that are specially designed to meet the needs of volunteer supervisors, consider starting a support group yourself. Again, contact such agencies and organizations as the local hospital, the Red Cross, and volunteer placement agencies to see if you can generate interest in developing a special interest group of people who manage volunteers in their workplace to exchange ideas and talk about special needs.

Finally, don't limit the development of your volunteer supervisor to workshops and programs that are specifically geared to volunteers. The management of volunteers, just like the management of any group of people, requires a wide range of skills in communication, delegation, training, and evaluation. Management workshops of any sort that are designed to address these and other personnel issues should be considered for your volunteer supervisor. If the program is to be successful, the person in charge should be kept abreast of ideas in management and should be encouraged to grow in her position as the valuable asset to the staff that she is.

Training Volunteers for Special Projects

Even libraries that don't have a regular volunteer workforce will depend on volunteer services when undertaking a special project that requires talents not available on staff or that requires lots and lots of help. Building projects, for example, will depend on special talents of volunteers when developing a building committee. Often the political skills of a person with a high community profile will be sought out, along with someone with legal skills, building skills, and perhaps a person with known negotiation skills. In addition, a building project is likely to require the help of many volunteers in putting together a "vote yes" campaign, a fund raising drive, and finally, to pack and move the collection.

Whatever your special need, volunteers who are recruited for a specific project that will take a finite period of time, will take some special management by your volunteer coordinator—who may, in fact, have been specially appointed for this project. Getting together large numbers of volunteers to work in concert for the completion of a project will usually take direct and on-going supervision by someone who is in charge. Even if only one person or a small committee of volunteers has been appointed to help with a special project, that person or committee will need direct supervision and feedback throughout the project to ensure that it is completed as planned.

A person who has been recruited because of the specific skills or experience she will be able to bring to a special library project will need to understand exactly how her skills are to be utilized. It's very important that expectations and time-lines are carefully laid out so that this volunteer understands exactly what the scope of her job is, what the anticipated results are and when the job needs to be completed. Without such a clear set of expectations, you may not get the results you planned and even if you do, they may come too late to be of value. On top of that, if a person has volunteered her valuable expertise and in the end you find it to be lacking because it wasn't timely or what you had expected, you will create some significant ill-will between this person and the library, always an unfortunate outcome.

When working with a volunteer who is lending special skills to a project, take the time needed in the very beginning to be clear about your expectations. Brainstorm with the volunteer to find out if her contributions will really net the library the results it wants. If you are clear about your goals and expectations, the volunteer will be able to help you ascertain whether or not she will be successful in helping you attain them. Be very clear about the project's time-line and work out a schedule that you both agree to with check points built in along the way where you agree to meet and go over progress.

Such a rigid schedule (which the volunteer supervisor is responsible for implementing) will ensure that the project is proceeding as planned and on time. These checkpoint meetings will keep the project on course and ensure a happy ending. It takes extra time and commitment from the volunteer coordinator, but if you are able to secure expert services for the library on a volunteer basis, it could well be worth it.

Often times, a special library project will require the assistance and management of a very large volunteer crew. Special fund raising campaigns, annual book sales, relocation of a large portion of the library's collection, or a special campaign to pass a library bond issue are all examples of times when the library needs to reach out to the community at large and pull together a temporary, but large, volunteer force. Obviously, the management of such a group will be time consuming and will require the constant oversight of a volunteer coordinator.

From the very beginning stages of a large volunteer project, a coordinator will be needed to analyze the need for volunteers and to design an implementation strategy so that volunteers can be organized and put to effective use. Once the the project has been well defined, a plan of how volunteers will be used in the accomplishment of the project must be developed. How many volunteers will be needed? How will they be organized and trained? When will they be needed and for how long? After putting the plan together, the recruitment process can begin. Using all likely avenues for recruitment (see Chapter 2), the volunteer coordinator can begin keeping a list of those who are willing and giving them a schedule for their work.

Throughout any large volunteer project which will be completed in a day or two such as a book sale or book moving, a supervisor will be needed on hand at all times. Volunteers will have questions throughout, they'll need to be kept on track and on task, and they'll have ideas on how to do it better. If you've done your planning well, discourage these—except for small and reasonable modifications. The midst of a large project involving a lot of volunteers is no time to start over, and if you're not there, someone else with a novel approach is likely to take charge! Volunteers working together on a big project are likely to need reinforcement and reassurance. It's wise to have someone responsible on hand at all times to see the project through to its successful completion.

If you are using volunteers for a special project that will take more than a day or two to complete, such as a fund raising project or political campaign, the volunteer coordinator will be needed to recruit and train volunteers and for setting up and attending meetings where goals are discussed and assignments given out. While in these cases, the volunteers will be more self-directed in their work than in a one or two day project, they will need guidance, training, and will need to attend check point meetings to discuss progress and develop on-going strategies.

It is likely and even desirable that in the case of a major fund raising campaign and especially in a political pro-library campaign, the volunteer coordinator is not a staff member. In this case it makes sense to assign the role of volunteer coordinator to a person who has demonstrated her ability to manage successfully longer term projects of a similar nature. There may be a suitable candidate in your Friends organization, among your patronage, or on the Board of Trustees. You may, in the case of a fund drive, choose to hire someone to direct the project.

However such a project and its volunteers are managed, it is critical to success that someone is clearly in charge. There should be someone visible and accessible who can clearly articulate the plan and can communicate to each volunteer how her work will contribute to its success. As with all special projects, a time-line should be set up and the volunteer coordinator should ensure that check points are in place so that the schedule and established procedures are being adhered to.

As anyone who has led a successful campaign that depended upon a lot of volunteers in the community will tell you, organizing, training, and keeping those volunteers on track is a full time job in itself. They will also tell you that when it's done right and well organized by someone who is clearly in charge, it's worth it!

Evaluations

Evaluations are an important part of any training and development program. Because evaluations can be an important tool for improvement and growth, they should be approached in a positive manner. Just as with paid staff, it makes sense to set up some kind of formal evaluation procedure and let your volunteers know what it is at the beginning of their employ. Will you give a written evaluation once a year? Will you take time out once a month to talk with them away from their workplace? Whatever method you use, you should be consistent and the volunteer should understand how and why the formal evaluation procedure will be conducted.

Even though this formal evaluation won't be linked to compensation as it often is with paid staff, it can be used in a similar way—to let your volunteers know how well they are doing, to share any concerns you may have for performance, to give volunteers an official avenue for making recommendations about their positions, and to give them an opportunity to let you know how they think the library management might make their jobs easier or more productive.

The first formal evaluation should be given after what could be considered the normal training period for a given position. If, for example, it normally takes four shifts to teach a volunteer how to cover books and a new volunteer comes in once a week to do so, you might schedule the first formal evaluation five weeks following the new volunteer's employ. This should give ample time for you to determine how well a volunteer's going to work in the position and the volunteer should be feeling fairly comfortable and confident.

As a positive tool, this evaluation is an opportunity to thank the volunteer in a formal and unhurried way. You can let her know how she's made a difference since coming on board. If you still observe some weaknesses in her performance, this is an opportunity to ask her if she could use some additional assistance or training in that area. Importantly, it's also a time to let her know how well you think she's doing. Spend time just talking about the job and how it's working out for the volunteer. Such a formal evaluation at this point shows the volunteer that she matters and the quality of her work matters.

Evaluations have gotten a bad rap. They shouldn't be a time of stress for either the volunteer supervisor or the volunteer. They should be looked upon as a time to touch base with each other in an unhurried manner, to share ideas about how to improve the job, the workflow, or the quality of the work. If handled sensitively and positively, the evaluation will be regarded by the volunteer as a reward reinforcing the fact that she matters, is valued, and makes a difference for the library.

Regardless of whether or not you set up official annual evaluations for your volunteer staff, you should be giving plenty of feedback on performance on a regular basis. So often, big mistakes or major misunderstandings about expectations can be avoided altogether if communication about performance is open and ongoing between supervisors and volunteers.

If you observe a volunteer making a small mistake, gently step in and lend a hand. Show her how you'd like it to be done. It can be uncomfortable to correct someone who's helping out from the goodness of her heart, but you're doing both the volunteer and yourself a favor if you correct small problems right away. Just to ensure that a sensitive volunteer isn't feeling bad about having been corrected, you might make an extra effort to be around at the end of her shift to let her know once again how much the library appreciates her help and how you look forward to seeing her next week.

Like formal evaluations, ongoing informal evaluation that consists of steady reinforcement should be looked at as a positive tool for development. When a volunteer is doing a good job, tell her so. You really can't do it too often. If you observe a volunteer making a good decision, handling a tricky situation well, coming up with an innovative approach to doing her job, let her know that you've noticed and it makes a difference. The more you are open and clear about the positive things a volunteer is doing, the easier it will be to make suggestions for improvement on the more negative aspects of her performance.

The quality of service that volunteers are able to provide depends so much on the quality of training and evaluation they receive. Good training takes a lot of time in the beginning but pays you back with self-directed, dependable volunteers in the long run. Evaluations, by comparison, take very little time and yet they, too, are key components to the development of the very best volunteer staff possible.

4

The "Challenging" Volunteer

Well here we are, at the very crux of the matter. We all know that "challenging" in this case is simply a kinder way of saying "problem" and, unfortunately, that's what some volunteers are—problems. He is that occasional volunteer who defies all tact, persuasion, training, and managerial cunning and who creates more difficulties, perhaps *far* more difficulties, than he and his contribution of time are worth. This hard-to-manage person causes us to rethink the very concept of volunteers. An extremely difficult volunteer problem can cause even the most patient of managers to question the value of volunteers and can make those managers who are dubious about the idea in the first place, firmly convinced that volunteers are indeed more trouble than they're worth.

It is virtually impossible to attend a workshop or conference on volunteers without hearing of at least one volunteer problem that can make even your finest management skills pale at the telling. The fact is, volunteers are different from paid staff. It is very difficult to use normal corrective methods with someone who is making a gift of his time; with someone who does not receive a paycheck— the very thing that makes paid staff members ultimately accountable for the quality of their work.

The special handling that is often required of those volunteers who truly do present troubling challenges is often more than managers are willing to take on. While an honest look at the big picture should make a most convincing argument for the overall benefits of volunteers, the occasional hair-raising story about the wayward volunteer can make the big picture seem pretty fuzzy and insignificant at times.

The trick, of course, is to find unique and sensitive ways of handling even the most perverse volunteer problem and to be sure that you are not creating the problem yourself by insufficient training and stifled lines of communication. The biggest trick of all, I believe, is to hang on to your sense of humor—perhaps the single most important asset for the successful management of volunteers.

Despite your very best efforts during the initial stages of "hiring" a volunteer, you are likely to find that you made a big mistake, that you have brought a volunteer on board who for one reason or another requires much more patience, time and tolerance than he is worth—by a long shot. When this happens to you (and it's likely to!), there *are* ways to cope.

In many cases, there is a solution that will work well for everyone. In some cases there is a solution that can at least be tolerated by everyone. Once in a while, however, you are likely to face a situation where nothing at all seems to work, nothing you have tried can turn an intolerable volunteer into a tolerable one. So, what's the answer? Can you actually fire a volunteer? In some special situations, that may in fact be the only reasonable course of action. There are, however, avenues to pursue before making such a radical, and perhaps unpopular, decision.

Back to Square One

Initial complacency by the supervisor may well be the cause of many volunteer "problems." Complacency can lead you to ignore the first signs that a volunteer isn't going to work out in the position you've assigned him. It is so important both for the quality of service a volunteer is able to give, and for good volunteer-management relations that you pay very close attention to any snags your volunteer hits (or creates!) when he first begins his work for you.

If you follow strict training procedures (see Chapter 3), you should have a very clear idea of how a volunteer is likely to do with a given job. If a volunteer isn't catching on in a reasonable amount of time, don't assume that he'll "get it" eventually. Even the smallest of problems can turn into big problems if left alone. Stay with a new volunteer until he demonstrates that he is fully capable of handling his job. If that just isn't happening, reassign him. It is much easier to try a volunteer out on a variety of tasks in the beginning until you find one that suits him than it is to reassign and retrain him later.

If you wait until a small problem escalates, you not only waste precious volunteer time, you will have to spend additional time getting things cleared up. Most importantly, you've allowed a situation to develop that will be likely to cause both you and the volunteer to feel uncomfortable. Rather than being in a position to explain to a volunteer that a job just doesn't seem to be suited to his skills (which is fairly easy and painless to do in the training stage), you will now be in a position of telling him what will sound to him like, "you blew it; you can't handle this job." Not a very pleasant situation.

The truth is, of course, that if initial placement and training weren't thorough, *you've* blown it. When you realize that truth it's likely to make you feel uncomfortable and you might even try to postpone the inevitable because of it. Even if you explain that training wasn't adequate, the volunteer may still feel that he didn't measure up.

If training, or lack of it, does seem to be the problem admit it and go back to square one. Begin at the beginning. Talk to the volunteer and ascertain whether or not he is happy in the position and feels that he can master the skills required for it. If he feels up to it and you are convinced that he is, agree to wipe the slate clean and start fresh. Analyze your training methods and try to find where they can be improved. As explained in the previous chapter, break the job down into its simplest components and train the volunteer one component of the job at a time. Do not move on until each component is mastered. This kind of careful training can be slow and painstaking but it is worth it if both you and the volunteer are convinced that inadequate training caused the problems.

If, on the other hand, either you or the volunteer is not convinced that better training will solve the problems, it's best to admit it at this point and discuss various other options open for volunteer service. It's important to be sure the volunteer knows that his service is still valued and appreciated and that the match was the problem—not him. Go back to the application form that he filled out for you. Ask questions about his past work experiences and his special talents and skills. Now that you know something more about what he can't do well, you may be able to ask better questions. What kinds of things has he done successfully in the past? What accomplishments does he feel most proud of?

In reassigning any volunteer, it becomes even more important that you don't make a mistake. Having to go through this *again* will be even harder and more uncomfortable for both of you. The best idea of all may be to reassign him to tasks that are extremely simple, letting him know that you will add to his responsibilities over time if this particular job is so easily accomplished by him that he feels it is too boring.

The truth of the matter is, if poor training or inappropriate placement was the problem, the solution is relatively simple even if somewhat embarrassing for you or the volunteer. It is those times when problems arise that are not related to training or placement that we face our real volunteer "challenges." It is these times when something more than remedial training or reassignment is necessary that volunteer supervisors really earn their stripes!

Some Typical "Challenges"

The Absent (What, Again?) Volunteer

Accountability. That's often the difficulty with volunteers. When you are not specifically hiring or paying someone because of his skills, but rather welcoming his gift of time, it is very hard to hold him accountable and this is probably most often true when it comes to schedules.

For most volunteers, work at the library is just a sideline in an otherwise busy life. Their work for you is probably not their top priority in life. Many volunteers lead busy and active lives. If they're retired, it is likely that they travel, have a variety of hobbies, or that they give their services to several agencies in town. When you combine a busy schedule with work at the library as a lower level priority in a volunteer's life, you know you will have a volunteer who will weigh some opportunities for leisure, service and travel above his commitment to the library. That's to be expected.

So how do you manage a volunteer work force that you depend upon to get work done but which is likely to be comprised of people who take off with much greater frequency than paid staff and certainly without feeling any need to ask for permission? You manage by understanding right up front that irregularity of scheduling is just part of the deal. That doesn't mean, however, that you can't take steps to ensure that volunteers give plenty of notice whenever possible and that you place those who take time off the most in positions where their absences won't cause a bottleneck in library service and operations.

Even though it's only fair to be tolerant and understanding of a volunteer's life apart from the library, you have every right and responsibility to set up a system of accountability. For example, if a volunteer is planning a six week trip to Tahiti, that's fine—you don't have a right to expect that trip to be scheduled around the library's needs. You *do* have the right to expect and require a fair amount of notice be given when such a trip is forthcoming.

On a day-to-day basis, you have every right to require that a volunteer who is unable to come in for his shift let you know as much in advance of his shift as possible. It is reasonable to expect that just as with your paid staff, illness or family emergency will mean that from time to time, a volunteer calls in at the last moment to let you know he isn't coming in. What is not reasonable is frequent last minute cancellation by a volunteer because something better has come up or because he just doesn't feel up to working today.

When it comes to accountability for meeting an agreed upon schedule, it is both fair and desirable to let the volunteer know that his value (as with all volunteers and employees) is greatly diminished if you feel he can't be counted on to come in when he says he will.

Of course, there may be the occasional volunteer who really wants to give some time to the library but just doesn't want to commit to a particular schedule. This is important information to get right in the beginning. If you have such a volunteer, you might assign a finite project that isn't too pressing and that can be done without supervision. If you bundle magazines for recycling, for example, or need to get a storage room cleaned up and organized, you might be able to use a responsible self-directed volunteer for such a project.

If you do take on a volunteer who will be coming and going at his convenience, realize that you will not be able to ensure that someone will be on hand to assist him, answer his questions, and supervise his work.

In these cases, it is very important that your initial training and instructions are very clear and that you are convinced that he is the kind of worker you can count on to follow through without any direct supervision. It would also be wise in such a situation, to set up some kind of system for touching base with him on a regular basis. Limit the hours he can come in to those when you are generally available, for example, and ask that he make it a point to check in with you (or your designee) each day he comes in before he begins his work. This way, you'll be able to let him know if he needs to modify his work, if there are other jobs you'd like him to tackle, or just to let him know that he's doing a great job and you're very glad he's able to help. It's also important for you to have some way of keeping track of the number of hours he is working for your records.

A lot of the frustration over the "absentee" volunteer can be eliminated if you realize that irregular attendance comes with the territory.

Realizing that, it makes sense to recruit and train a few volunteers in a variety of tasks who are willing to work "on call." Many of your best volunteers can be easily taught a variety of functions and it is likely that there are several among them who would be willing and even flattered to be called in on a substitute basis when another volunteer can't make it. Keep a list of potential substitute volunteers and add to it at every opportunity.

Even if you can't hold volunteers to a strict schedule with a limited number of vacation and sick days, you can help them see that their service to you matters enough that it makes a difference when they're gone. No volunteer will find it unreasonable that rules have been put in place regarding notice for vacations. Furthermore, it is important that you let them know that if they commit to a schedule, they should feel responsible for meeting it. It is also reasonable to expect that from time to time something important will come up that prevents their coming to work. All volunteers should realize from the start, however, that if you cannot depend upon their commitment to an agreed upon schedule, it will limit the number of positions that they will be qualified to assume in the library.

Almost Perfect, But Not Quite

It seems to me that more often than not, a conversation about "challenging" volunteers by their supervisors will begin something like this: "Tim is a wonderful volunteer, he's willing to come in several times a week to shelve books and he is extremely accurate and conscientious but. . . ." (here it comes), "Tim just doesn't understand the limits of his job. He's always stopping his work to help patrons, answer the phone, and I've even caught him trying to answer reference questions."

The truth is, some of the best volunteers tend to reach beyond acceptable boundaries to take on inappropriate tasks. If you ask Tim's supervisor why he doesn't confront Tim directly and explain that serving patrons or answering the phone is outside the realm of his job, you would be likely to get the response that the supervisor is afraid of alienating Tim and risk losing an otherwise exceptional volunteer.

I know of one case where the almost perfect volunteer was indeed taking time from her shelving duties in the children's room to offer reader's advisory service and attempting to tackle reference questions. The supervisor tried to redirect the volunteer back to her own work by telling her gently but firmly that she wasn't expected to help the patrons; that the staff was there for that and this volunteer shouldn't feel obligated to interrupt her own work to help them.

It probably isn't too surprising that the volunteer never got the hint. In fact, when told that she didn't "need" to interrupt her work to serve patrons her response was, "I don't mind a bit, it's actually the best part of working at the library." Once the volunteer has had an opportunity to convey that she likes serving patrons best and clearly feels qualified to do so, it becomes doubly hard to reign her in and restrict her to the volunteer tasks which you've assigned.

The best way to avoid a situation where an otherwise terrific volunteer begins to take on more than he is really qualified or required to do and, in fact, is interfering with the work of paid staff, is with a clear job description and good one-on-one training in the beginning of the volunteer's employ which emphasizes the importance of staying on task and makes it clear that he is required to get permission before spreading his wings.

Even with good initial training and with clear job descriptions, a good volunteer who can easily and accurately perform the tasks assigned is likely to gain confidence and begin taking on more and more responsibility over time. At first, the assumption of new duties might be so gradual (and perhaps initially appreciated) that you are reluctant to say anything. The fact is, if a volunteer is taking on more and inappropriate responsibility, it could well be a sign that his volunteer job just isn't fulfilling enough and it needs to be enhanced—by the supervisor, not by the volunteer.

In the case of Tim, for example, the best solution probably is the direct one. Sitting down with Tim, the supervisor could explain that while often Tim's advise to patrons is exactly right, the possibility is genuine that without professional assistance, a patron might leave without getting the information he wants even if the library has it on hand. A clear but simple explanation that staff members know the collection well enough to turn up those hard to find answers and that patrons themselves often don't ask the right questions to get what they need, should help Tim see that his service to patrons could be detrimental.

Once you get past the hard part (letting Tim know that he is not to take on reader's advisory and reference) discuss with him some of the options for enhancing his job at the library to make it more meaningful and fun. Perhaps he can produce booklists the library staff has put together, or work with the youth services librarian in getting materials together for storytimes.

Almost perfect volunteers are extremely valuable assets. It's important that they never doubt our appreciation for their contribution. Even terrific volunteers must be told if there is an aspect of their performance that isn't acceptable. Doing so in a sensitive manner with options for their growth within the organization is the best way to enhance their value to the library and protect their dignity as well.

The Know It All

There is a difference between providing fresh perspective and trying to run the place. You and I know that, but once in awhile you will get a volunteer who doesn't know that. On occasion, you are likely to get a volunteer whose background is in business administration—or worse yet, in library administration! If you can't tactfully send them off to the Red Cross or the hospital gift shop, you will have to do the next best thing: be extremely clear about the limits of their responsibilities and put them someplace where their expertise will be helpful but not desperately needed.

I have a friend who retired after many years in administration for special libraries. In an effort to fill his newfound leisure time (and donate the benefit of his vast library management experience to the community), he volunteered for service at his local public library.

Initially, the volunteer coordinator at this public library was delighted. My friend (I'll call him Bill) is charming, intelligent, capable, and hard working. Who wouldn't like to have benefit of his talent and expertise—for free?

As Bill tells the story, this public library had just passed a bond issue for the expansion and remodeling of their facility and because Bill had charge of two building programs during his library tenure, he was assigned a position on the "relocation" team. The job of this team was to determine how the collection would be moved from its current location to its new location when the time was right. They would not only devise the plan, but they would solicit the community volunteer help needed to implement the plan.

"Right away," Bill told me, "I knew they were making some big mistakes with their floor plans. I felt the public service areas were taking up too much space where shelving could go. Not only that, but they were planning to move the Children's Room up out of the basement and locate it on the main floor of the library! No matter how many times I discussed these obvious problems with the director, the plans stayed more or less the same."

What Bill will go on to say is that his point of view was greatly colored by his work in special libraries. In addition to that, he said he often feels that his points of disagreement with the director boiled down to ego—Bill simply felt that the library should defer to his experience and expertise. "I never stopped trying to run the place," Bill said. "I just couldn't help it. Sometimes I was right in my opinion, often I was wrong. The point was, it wasn't *my* library. Finally the volunteer coordinator gave me the boot and sent me, along with a good recommendation, to a local nursing home where I now read to and discuss literature with interested residents every Tuesday afternoon. I love it. And if things aren't managed appropriately, that's not my problem!"

Lucky for this library Bill has both a sense of humor and perspective. Unfortunately, that's not always the case. One thing even Bill agrees with, however, is that when a volunteer is interfering with the very management of an institution because he thinks he can do it better, it's probably time for him to go. It is not likely in this case that Bill could have happily been reassigned or that it would have made any difference in his compulsion to give input.

Perhaps Bill is the extreme in the case of volunteers who always have a better way to do it. And truthfully, volunteers, like other library staff members, sometimes *do* have a better way to do it.

The problem comes when a particular volunteer is regularly and emphatically giving the library the benefit of his superior wisdom. Based on past experience, this over-zealous volunteer is likely to want to impose his management style and structure on your organization. In addition to wanting to get him to ease off with the suggestions that are both regular and emphatic, you may want to retain him as a valuable volunteer.

As is so often the case, the best approach may well be the direct approach. If you have a volunteer who is self-confident and assertive enough to want to dramatically change the library's operations, it is unlikely that he will be overly sensitive when you explain to him that his "suggestions" are interfering with management of the library and are therefore, not productive. Be clear that you did not bring him aboard because of his management expertise, but for his ability to do the job you've assigned. Ask him if he can understand your concerns and if he can be happy working solely within the limitations of his appointed position.

If you feel that this volunteer does in fact have something to contribute but you do want to curb his zeal a bit, you might try developing some less direct avenues of input for him. Require, for example, that he put his requests in writing and let him know that you will discuss with him any of those ideas which you feel have merit and possibility. Be clear in letting him know that it is counterproductive for him to request discussion and debate over each idea or concept. "Don't call me, I'll call you" should be the bottom line of this compromise.

The Innovative Volunteer

Some volunteers will not come to you with their ideas about how the library might be managed better, some volunteers will simply take it upon themselves to do something. While I cannot honestly say I've heard of a volunteer who went so far, for example, as to reshelve books according to color or size, I do know that there are volunteers who see a better way of doing something and then just do it.

Making sure that volunteers stay within the scope of their position and perform their duties as trained can sometimes be a challenge itself. Volunteers who are self-starters and self-directed can be among your best volunteers. Often they are easy to train and require very little remedial assistance. In short, you can depend on them — a real plus. Volunteers who are self-directed, however, may well be inclined from time to time, to take on more than their assigned duties simply because they see work that needs to be done and. . . they know a great way to do it!

A friend of mine who is the director of a small library in an old and historic town told me of a case where she had found a volunteer who was willing to index all the local history magazines going back to the mid–1800s. No other index for these magazines existed and the librarian knew that an index for them would open access to a real wealth of information for local history buffs and for kids doing homework assignments on the history of their town.

After setting up a file on a very simple computer database program, the librarian spent several sessions working with the volunteer explaining how to use keywords to determine subjects, and how to create a thesaurus and a cross reference file so that access would be uniform. It was clear within a short period of time that this volunteer, a history buff herself, had a keen sense of subject and could easily determine what information was important for the index and what wasn't. The volunteer was a godsend, the index she produced would literally unlock the treasures of over one hundred years of articles written about their town and state. Not only that, the thesaurus the volunteer was creating would allow future librarians or volunteers to continue to index local magazines and pamphlets.

Even after she had determined that this volunteer was competent to proceed on her own, the librarian continued to check from time to time during the course of the next week or two and was convinced that all was well. At that point, the librarian did no more than to ask the volunteer at the end of each shift how it was going. It wasn't until the project was completed about six months later that the librarian discovered a *major* problem.

Somewhere along the line, it occurred to the volunteer that since all the records had to do with either "Ourtown" or Massachusetts, it would make sense to go back and indicate before each subject heading that the subject was indeed "Ourtown" or Massachusetts. She entered the town name or state right before the subject on the same field line. What this meant was that the computer couldn't sort the subjects in alphabetical order — they were all sorted by either "Massachusetts — Smith, John" or by Ourtown — Smith, John."

"At first, I panicked," my friend told me. "All that work, six months! And the index looked entirely useless." After calming down a bit, the librarian realized that it would be fairly simple and quick to go through the file and simply remove the town and state name and resort the file — now in alphabetical order by subject. The point is, the potential for disaster is always there if volunteers decide to innovate.

While this librarian did a good job in training and even did some periodic checking, somehow the volunteer felt free to change the format of the file. Innovative changes can be made in an instant and take hours or days to remedy. Periodic checking on a volunteer's progress may not be enough. Once again, it is vitally important that volunteers are extremely clear about the boundaries of their work. Let them know right up front that you want them to perform their duties *exactly* as you've trained them. Let them know that while you value innovation, it must be cleared with you first. No matter how small or insignificant a volunteer may feel a change is, they must clearly understand and appreciate that small changes can sometimes cause big problems.

Beware the Volunteer Bearing Gifts

This is a true story. I was the director of a library many years ago that depended heavily on the services of volunteers. Because we were active in the recruitment, training, and placement of volunteers, we hired a volunteer coordinator to manage them. The woman we hired (Beth) possessed the most important qualifications needed to successfully manage a large and diverse volunteer staff—patience, tact and humor. None of these three qualities, however, were enough to see her through when one volunteer decided to stretch his creative wings.

One day Beth came into my office with her hands behind her back and a look of sheer disbelief on her face. "You'll never guess what Carol has done now." (Carol, by the way was known for her unique but usually harmless innovations for service.) "Guess, just guess, what she's done." After telling Beth I couldn't possibly guess, she brought her hands from around her back and said, "Look at these, can you believe it? We're supposed to give these to our patrons with a straight face?"

What Beth had to show me were two homemade bookmarks, one was a very large pink heart and the other a blue car. "She's made hundreds of these and she's handing the pink ones out to all our female patrons, and the blue ones to our male patrons." Not only was the concept fairly sexist, Carol's generous spirit far exceeded her artistic talents. The bookmarks were certainly not attractive and to make matters worse, Carol had inscribed each bookmark with the slogan "Compliments of Ourtown Library: Have a Nice Day"—capped off with a smiley face! "I can't let her continue to hand these out," Beth stated. "They're ugly, sexist, and they certainly do nothing to enhance the professional image we're trying to develop. I just don't know what to tell Carol, she's *so* proud, she worked so hard on these."

After some discussion about possible solutions (and after I stopped laughing!), we decided management by subterfuge was our best route. This was a sensitive situation indeed. We couldn't see anyway of withdrawing those bookmarks without hurting Carol's feelings. What we decided to do was let her go for the rest of the shift then dispose of the remaining bookmarks immediately. We told Carol when she came to work the following week that we had given out all the bookmarks and that her bookmarks gave us the idea of having a bookmark contest for children, so we wouldn't need any more.

In order to make up the loss to Carol (yes, we did feel guilty), we consulted with Carol about the possibility of her taking charge of the bookmark contest. We asked Carol to make rules for the contest, publicize it, and select among all our volunteers a commit-tee to judge the winners. Then we put Carol in charge of getting the bookmarks printed up. All this was done with the approval and under direct supervision of the youth services librarian. Finally, we asked that Carol let us know in advance if she had any other ideas for promotion so that we could work together on implementing them.

It was a simple, and (now) humorous incident but it had im-plications for a volunteer's dignity. Carol felt that she was helping to promote the library in a special and personal way. While Carol was expecting kudos, her supervisor was up in my office tearing her hair out. To be honest, the innovation that some volunteers bring to the library without prior consultation with their supervisor can be the trickiest volunteer issues to deal with.

The moral of this story, is that sometimes there is no perfect solution. It is important, however, that when solutions are found for volunteer problems, they respect the dignity of the volunteer con-cerned. Volunteers feel that the gifts of their time and their talents are valuable and we need to respect that. There are times when honesty is not the best policy, times when we must tactfully redirect a volunteer's talents in a direction that will honor those talents and serve the library as well.

While Carol's gift came unexpectedly and uninvited, there are times when you might well ask a volunteer with special talent to make something for the library. Quality control is important in these cases. Realize that if you give *carte blanche* to a volunteer to design and produce furniture or equipment you will find it difficult indeed to reject their gift if it doesn't meet your expectations or re-quirements. When Carol was redirected to take charge of a book-mark contest, she did so under the close supervision of the youth services librarian who was able to ensure that all went well and that there was some quality control.

In the end, the best solution may be to discourage volunteer "gifts" altogether unless the volunteer is an expert craftsperson with whose work you are very familiar. Even then, be absolutely clear about what you want and set up checkpoints all through design and production so that you can control the outcome of the product. When a gift is a surprise, produced with a loving heart for the library; be gentle, be creative, and redirect that volunteer's efforts as quickly and effectively as possible!

The Aging Volunteer

Volunteers who are simply incapable of doing their jobs can often be retrained or moved into another, easier position in the library. Once in awhile, however, a volunteer grows incompetent over time without really realizing it and in these cases, retraining or reassignment are not always easy solutions.

Many of our volunteers are people of retirement age. They come to us because they have now have extra time in their lives and want to make a contribution to the community. It is probably safe to say that retired people make up the backbone of libraries' volunteer force. We owe them a lot. Occasionally, aging volunteers begin to forget things, take a lot of time to accomplish a simple task, and slowly grow incompetent. If you have a volunteer who has worked for the library for a long time in a particular position, it is likely that moving him to another job in the library will not be easy. When the volunteer is moved to a new and easier position after serving well in another position, he will surely feel that you are "demoting" him. He's worked in the library long enough to understand that there are some volunteer activities that are reserved for those who might otherwise "screw things up." It's probable that you won't be fooling him a bit if you tell him that you need his help in another, less demanding, area.

It is difficult to imply that a person's value to the library has diminished as his age has increased. It is a tough situation for both you and the volunteer. It is likely that over time you've grown fond of this long-time volunteer. He's given so much to the library. You and the community are in his debt. On the other hand, you've got a library to run, tasks to accomplish, service to provide to a demanding and often impatient public. Are you doing your job if you allow an incompetent individual to remain in place? What about the mistakes being made; what kind of impact are they having on the work of other staff members? What kind of impact are his increasing mistakes having on service?

The reality is that the aging process can mean a deterioration in both mental and physical abilities and this fact will sometimes affect the quality of work by a volunteer. When a volunteer "problem" is as personal and sensitive as this, it requires a personal and sensitive approach. The best solution for each case will probably be as unique as the individual himself.

When you have a long-time volunteer who is having increasing difficulty in performing his job, try to determine, based on what you know of him, what the best approach will be to discuss the problem—if you feel he's aware of the increasing mistakes too, sometimes he's not. It may be that together you can come up with a solution. You might, for example, try to put some of the "blame" for the increasing errors on the fact that the library has become so much busier and work routines, more complex. Ask him if there is anything you can do to make the job easier. If he's open to the fact that his work is slipping, it might just be possible to suggest a lateral move and he might be relieved.

On the other hand, the volunteer may feel that he's doing as well as ever and is unwilling to admit that his work is slipping. It may be a matter of personal pride and an unwillingness to recognize that some deterioration in his capabilities have set in that will make him seem stubborn and make your task harder. If this is the case, you might try taking a good look at the job and considering if, indeed, his slower pace and mistakes matter all that much. Is it possible, for example, to find another volunteer to work a shift immediately following his to go over his work, fixing mistakes and completing anything left unfinished?

If this volunteer is working alone in a position where his mistakes will not be found until they've caused bigger problems (shelving for example, or checking books in), you might consider finding him a partner. Rather than implying that his work needs "watching," you could tell him that due to increasing use of the library, you are instituting a "double check" system for all positions where even a few errors can cause bigger problems. This, too, may not go over well with an independent volunteer who feels that if his work has always been fine in the past, it's certainly fine now. Whether he likes it or not, however, you *do* in fact have a job to do and quality to ensure, and this tactic may be the kindest approach.

One librarian told me that she had an aging volunteer who was more than "slipping." This volunteer was the unfortunate victim of Alzheimer's disease. "This particular volunteer had worked for me for many years and she told me often that working at the library was the highlight of her week. How could I kick her when she was down? How could I add to her distress by taking away something she loved so much—work at the library?" In this case, the librarian told me, a lateral move was possible and the woman suffering from the disease, at least in the initial stages, was able to shelve picture books which had been presorted and stacked for her. She required a lot of attention by the staff because she needed constant reminders about her job, but the staff knew the situation was temporary (she wouldn't be with them long) and they cared about her. Together they worked out a system where the volunteer could do little harm with the least disruption of other staff members.

In the end, sensitivity and thoughtfulness will probably see you through most of these special cases. Having a good sense of priority helps. Are the mistakes that important? Is the extra time needed to give direction and support that disruptive? It also helps to be creative. Can the job be subtly restructured to minimize the damage the volunteer might do? Would it help to bring in a "partner" who will serve as a quality control measure as well as support?

In my mind, volunteers who have given years of service to the library are extra special—they deserve extra special consideration from us when and if the time comes.

The Personality's the Problem

Sometimes it's simply the personality. . . or not so simply! In fact, if personality *is* the problem, it may be a very difficult one to deal with. If you have a large volunteer force, you have a wide variety of personalities to contend with. While this diversity is often what makes the job so enriching and fulfilling, occasionally a person will come along who quite simply drives you all crazy. It's not that he does anything wrong, exactly. It's just that for one reason or another he's no fun to be around.

I hired a volunteer once who, after raising a large family, was very anxious to get into the "working world." This woman (I'll call her Ethel) had never held a job outside the home before and volunteer work at the library seemed like the perfect place to start. Ethel was able and willing to work ten hours a week and she didn't care what work was assigned to her. I was thrilled. After going over her application, it was clear that while she had no formal work experience, she did raise a large family. She would have a lot of life skills, right?

We began with a simple filing job. It took a little longer than

I expected because Ethel had a hard time differentiating between letter by letter filing as opposed to word by word filing and was inclined to mix them indiscriminately. No problem, I'd just spend a little more time with her — she'd pick it up. Well, it wasn't that Ethel was incapable of picking it up, she just wouldn't concentrate long enough for me to explain things. Ethel was a talker. Not only that, but her conversations were often odd and completely out of context with what we were in the middle of discussing. For example, she'd go off into a discussion about her new granddaughter and then stop right in the middle and say something like, "I needlepoint." Hmmmm.

Well, eventually Ethel picked up on the filing rules and though slightly slow, she was competent enough at it. I thought that if I stayed out of her way, she'd be able to finish the filing without too much conversation and we could move onto training for another task.

It wasn't long before other staff members and volunteers began filtering into my office. "What's the deal with Ethel," they'd ask. "She comes into our areas and goes into these long discussions. She'll even interrupt our conversations, interjecting something that has nothing whatever to do with what we're talking about. You can't even pass her in the hall without her engaging you in a conversation."

Okay, the solution here is simply to talk to Ethel and let her know that she has to stick to the task. In fact, I was very clear about how long I felt any non-work related conversation should last. "No more than two minutes," I told her. I realized that without any workplace skills, she needed clear-cut guidelines; she simply didn't know what was appropriate and she wanted to be one of the gang.

As time when on, I found that everyone was more or less avoiding Ethel. They'd leave the break room shortly after she'd come in, for example. When passing her in a hall or workroom, others would avert their heads and avoid conversations with her. To be honest I felt sorry for Ethel. But there was something distinctly eccentric about her. She seemed totally incapable of holding a normal conversation with people. It wasn't that she was rude or mean, it was just that she had no social skills; interrupting people with non sequitors, for example.

When complaints started coming in that Ethel's clothing and breath smelled so heavily of tobacco that co-workers found it offensive, I knew I had a real problem. Other people on staff smelled of tobacco too, but no one was complaining about them. The staff was launching a not so subtle attempt to get rid of Ethel. They really didn't have anything concrete to refer to in not liking her, so they latched on to the tobacco odor as a way to complain.

I was truly torn. I felt about Ethel pretty much the way the staff did, and yet she was a competent enough worker and really hadn't done anything wrong. Diversity and tolerance, those are the words I'd whisper to myself whenever I thought about Ethel. How could I continue to use Ethel as a volunteer (she was really enjoying her work, she told me), and yet not have mutiny among the rest of the staff?

Luckily, Ethel hadn't been locked into any particular job and was learning a variety of tasks. I was able to find a job that she enjoyed and that kept her away from other staff members. Working in a small office, Ethel was put in charge of our local archives. She sorted and clipped all news items about the library and even prepared a sort of index so that they could be accessed. She was also put in charge of bundling newspapers for recycling and bundling discarded magazines. These jobs filled her week and though she still interacted with staff on breaks and occasionally in the halls, she was more or less on her own.

Meanwhile, the rest of us focused on diversity and tolerance at an all-staff meeting. We talked about the need to honor different work styles and different personalities. In time, Ethel improved her social skills, the staff began to feel more comfortable with her and it seemed to work out for everyone.

Some personalities are more than vaguely disconcerting, however. Some are downright grumpy. How does this happen? Why does someone who *volunteers* to work at the library, seem so very unhappy at being there? Anyone who has managed volunteers for any length of time has certainly come across the grumpy volunteer.

This is the volunteer who never smiles, snaps out answers to questions, and often complains about his work. A grumpy volunteer, just like a grumpy staff member, is bad medicine for everyone.

Nothing, I think, is more contagious than a bad attitude. People who seem perennially unhappy with life in general seem to be able to bring happy people down far more easily than the other way around. In fact, happy people often seem to make grumpy people grumpier!

So what can you do with a volunteer who has a bad attitude? In this case, confront him. It's too serious a problem to ignore, and you never know, there may actually be a reason the volunteer is so unhappy—and it may be something that you can fix. You would think grown people would let you know directly if something is wrong, but that's not always the case. Some people will let you know indirectly by muttering under their breath, making generally disparaging comments, heaving great sighs at all requests made of him, and by snapping at others.

If you have a volunteer acting this way consistently, pull him aside. Ask him if he's comfortable and happy in his volunteer position. Ask if there's anything you can do to make his job easier. At this point, the volunteer might let you know about grievances real or perceived which he's been harboring and letting fester. Some of the issues you may well be able to do something about; some may simply be in the nature of the job in which case you could discuss a lateral move to a position he likes better.

On the other hand, the grumpy volunteer may tell you everything's just fine. If so, you must tell him that you have observed behavior that made you feel he wasn't happy. Then, *be specific.* What exactly have you observed? If he's snapped at co-workers or patrons, tell him when and where. If he mutters and complains, tell him that's what you've observed and give examples. This is likely to be a tough conversation to conduct, so make it count. Don't back down by being vague. If you do, he's likely to deny that there's any problem with his behavior.

Be sure to temper your discussion with the fact that you value his contribution to the library (if, in fact, you do) but let him know that the behaviors you've observed cannot continue in the workplace. Let him know that others are affected when someone's attitude is grumpy and complaining. Yes, it's true, if you're this direct with this volunteer there's a chance he'll quit. No matter how valuable his contributions may be otherwise, it is not fair to others who must work with him to let this behavior continue. In the end, you're likely to pay the biggest price with a formerly happy staff who now seems to be complaining and grumpy more often than not.

Truly Terrible Volunteer Problems

Paradoxically, the real big problems with volunteers may be the easiest to deal with precisely because they are so big. Whereas many volunteer challenges stem from behavior and difficulties that are not really earth-shattering (therefore easy to rationalize ignoring), major problems that are obvious to everyone demand quick and decisive action and usually it will be clear to you and everyone else what action to take.

Stealing, for example, obviously can't be tolerated and depending on the amount taken, your job is to fire the culprit and possibly to press charges. Basically, this is a pretty cut-and-dried situation. Of course *suspecting* a volunteer of stealing is a more difficult challenge and requires careful monitoring and perhaps reassignment to another area to see if the theft stops. If you can't prove a volunteer is stealing but feel fairly certain he is, reassign him to a position where he is monitored at all times and perhaps one that is no fun. In the best case he'll quit; at worst he is under observation and away from temptation at all times. In the end, if you can't prove he's stealing, it would be very risky for you to take action as though you could—firing him on that suspicion, for example.

Other "big" problems have to do with overt behavior that you wouldn't tolerate from other staff members: foul language, gross rudeness to patrons, sexual harassment, or harassment of others in general. Behavior that crosses the line of acceptability should not be allowed of anyone. If you have a volunteer who is exceeding the bounds of acceptable behavior, harassing or picking fights with other workers, using foul language offensive to all others, you have to take action. It might be best to give one firm and unequivocal warning, or it might be best to fire him outright. You have to use the same good judgment you'd use with other staff members. Realize, however, that if you allow a volunteer to continue to engage in behavior that is legally actionable, sexual harassment for example, you too could be held legally liable if you knowingly allow it to continue.

Some major problems are obvious to everyone and yet are a little more difficult to handle. Specifically, behavior that can't be tolerated but that may be beyond the volunteer's ability to control is a case in point. Alcohol or drug addiction may seriously impair an otherwise good person and volunteer and if the incidents are occasional, that can make the solution harder.

A fellow librarian, Mary, told me the story of a volunteer who was an alcoholic. "She wasn't drinking when I hired her and she only goes on binges once in awhile . . . they do seem to be happening with more frequency, though," Mary told me. To make matters worse, this volunteer was recommended to Mary by a board member who said that working for the library would do this volunteer a world of good. Ominous words! When the volunteer was recommended to Mary she was quite happy to take her on, especially since the volunteer had excellent typing skills—something this small library greatly needed.

On the drinking days, this volunteer could barely set the tabs on the typewriter, let alone be expected to competently type anything. On top of that, the aroma of alcohol was often strong enough that patrons in the area could smell it. Worst of all, the volunteer would drive to and from work in a state of intoxication.

My friend Mary didn't really know what to do. When the volunteer was sober, she was a real asset to the staff. When she was drunk, she was useless.

Because the drinking episodes were fairly infrequent (though increasing), Mary simply redirected her work to something simple like picking up magazines and books left on tables and bringing them to circulation to be reshelved. She felt an obligation to her trustee who recommended the volunteer, and she, too, felt that the structure of the volunteer job was helping her to keep her drinking to a minimum.

We all make the best choices that we can in tough situations. I think I would be far less tolerant if I were in Mary's position, however. For one thing, letting someone remain at work in a state of intoxication sets a bad precedent. You can't allow a volunteer to do something that you would never accept of a staff member. Secondly, if the volunteer smells of alcohol and is allowed to be anywhere near patrons, you're certainly changing the image of library staff—in a very unfavorable way! Finally, the act of sanctioning, however passively, drunk driving by allowing a person under the influence of alcohol to come to work means you are playing a part in a potential disaster. It may be true that if the drunk volunteer wasn't driving to the library she'd be driving someplace else, but there's no way to be sure of that. The best you can do (and the most responsible thing you can do) is to be sure she isn't driving on your account—to get to work for you.

I believe that the volunteer who comes to work drunk should be driven home immediately with the firm understanding that she must be sober to come to and work at the library. I would even follow up with a phone call the next day or the next until you are able to have a sober conversation. The volunteer should know that if she chooses to drink she must stay home, that her services at the library won't be welcome as long as she's drinking. In the long run, you don't help anyone by accommodating their drinking in any way, and you certainly don't help the library by allowing intoxicated volunteers or staff members to be at the library.

Finally, the trustee who recommended this volunteer should be contacted. Did the trustee know that the volunteer had a drinking problem? That was certainly implied by the comment that work at the library would do this person "a world of good." If the trustee did know of the problem, it's important for him to know that the library isn't the place for rehabilitation. It should be made diplomatically clear to the trustee that both your and his first responsibility is to the good of the library, not the good of the volunteer. If the trustee was unaware of the problem, letting him know is fine. If this volunteer was a friend of his maybe the trustee could do something (other than finding volunteer work for her!) to help.

From the perspective of the library, the bottom line is clear: substance abuse and library work do not mix. It is important that this message is unequivocal and that it is equally enforced for all people working at the library; whether they are paid or not.

Keeping Perspective

The "challenging" volunteers are the ones who make us wonder why on earth we ever opened the doors to volunteers in the first place. It's not that you don't care about them as people—you do! That's why making it work matters so much to you, that's why the "challenging" volunteer gets under your skin in the first place.

For every problem volunteer, there's probably a slightly different solution. Volunteer management is far more art than science. The best you can do to keep volunteer problems to a minimum is to invest heavily in their training, support and evaluation. If you don't have time to invest at this end, you don't have time to manage volunteers. Realize that and make a case for the financial support necessary to make a volunteer force the asset that it can and should be. Don't take on more than you can realistically handle, because volunteers won't lighten your load if they are not well trained.

Perhaps most important of all for the successful management of volunteers is a sense of both humor and perspective. Yes, the occasional problem volunteer will make you crazy for awhile. When you solve the problem, however, you'll feel great—you'll feel confident that you're a good manager and that you are handling well a job that makes a real difference in your community. You are helping the library stretch its budget and you are enriching the lives of people who work for you.

The "challenging" volunteer is the exception. By far, most people who offer their services to the library enrich its services beyond simply the number of hours they are able to give. They reinforce for everyone who works at the library that library service is so important to the community they're willing to give their time and efforts to it. They can bring diversity and fresh perspectives. They will be your best advocates when you need them, and best of all, they do indeed lighten the work load for everyone.

5

Saying "Thank You"

When you take time each year to add up the number of hours that have been donated to the library by volunteers; when you take a moment to imagine what library service in your community would be like without the time and support that volunteers give; you may well be overwhelmed by the sheer magnitude of their gift. Volunteers not only allow us to enhance and improve the service our patrons use and appreciate, they enable staff to find sanity in a storm of increasing demand brought on by growing popularity and a changing technological world. Volunteers tell us by their mere presence that our jobs are so important and worthwhile that they'll help us do them—for free! How can we ever thank them?

In truth, for most volunteers, working for the community through the library is its own reward. Altruism is surely the greatest motivator. Nevertheless, it is incumbent upon all of us who enjoy a lightened load because of volunteers to find ways to let them know how much we appreciate their service. In big ways and small ways, it is important for us to say thanks and to let them know that they make a difference.

Recognition and Awards

People who make a difference in the community are entitled to recognition for it. The act of giving recognition shows that a volunteer's time and effort matters a lot to you and your library. In addition, public recognition reminds members of your community

With Grateful Appreciation

This certificate is awarded to

_____

For outstanding contribution to the

Anycity Public Library

through _____ *hours of volunteer service.*

ANYCITY
Official
SEAL
PUBLIC LIBRARY

_____
President, Board of Trustees

_____
Director, Anycity Public Library

_____
Date

Design by Shelley Countryman; Macintosh LC III; Aldus Freehand 3.0; Fonts: Regency Script & Palatino.

that they, too, benefit from the services of their fellow citizens who are working to improve the quality of life in their town. In fact, public recognition of existing volunteers may be your very best recruiting tool because it lets others know that there are volunteer opportunities at the library and that the library is grateful for the help.

There is an infinite variety of ways to give recognition—limited only by your imagination, and not by your pocketbook.

Certificates of Appreciation

A very simple but effective way to let volunteers know how much they mean to you and the library is to give them a special "Certificate of Appreciation." These certificates can be simple, purchased through a local stationery supply store, or they can be a little more special. It is not difficult to design certificates in-house using the artistic talents of a staff member or to design certificates using desktop publishing then having them mass produced on special paper by a local printing company (see examples on page 98 and below). In fact, designing a special certificate might be a volunteer job itself.

Used with permission.

There may be someone in your community who has artistic talent who would be willing to design a very special certificate. If there is an artist in your community with a national, regional or even local reputation, you might convince her to design a special certificate using the talents in her particular field (graphic arts, illustration, watercolor, oils) which could be printed in limited editions (for volunteers only), numbered and signed by the artist. That way the certificate not only commemorates the service given by the volunteer but becomes a keepsake as well—suitable for framing!

Certificates of appreciation can be used to recognize length of service in addition to recognizing service alone. If you are able to get an artist to number and sign printed editions of her work, for example, you could give those volunteers with the greatest years of service, the lowest print numbers. Whatever certificates you design or buy, it makes sense to recognize those who have been with you for many years. You might put a special gold seal on the certificates of those who have been with you for over five years or use gold and silver frames to commemorate years of service.

There are also those volunteers who do something extra special and noteworthy. The person who has put together and managed an entire team to inventory the collection, for example. In cases where someone has clearly gone above and beyond the call of duty, a special certificate recognizing that achievement will mean a lot to the recipient.

Tell It to the Press

Libraries are pretty savvy about using the press to tout their services, announce upcoming events, or simply to talk about library issues that affect everyone. Why not use this effective outlet to let your community know how much it benefits from volunteers at the library? An annual press release telling about the different volunteer opportunities at the library, the number of hours each year that volunteers donate, and that gives the names of those who have volunteered throughout the year will be an effective way of giving recognition and of highlighting library volunteer services in general. (See example on page 101.)

SAMPLE VOLUNTEER PRESS RELEASE

For Immediate Release
April 10, 1994

From: Sue Smith, Director
of Volunteer Services
Anycity Public Library
123-4567

Volunteer Hours Top 7,500 at the Anycity Public Library

282 volunteers gave over 7,500 hours of service to the Anycity Public Library this year, the highest number of hours contributed in the library's history.

"The library is often cited as the best service in town," said John Jones, library director. "The high quality of service that we are able to provide would not be possible without the generous contribution of time and talent by our library volunteers. While it's hard to imagine replacing this great and dedicated group at any price, we know that at the very least it would cost our community over $65,000 a year to pay for their services."

This year, the library will be giving special recognition to Deb Martin, Bill Johnson, and Betty Watson for their years of service. Each of these three volunteers has worked at the library for over fifteen years. "I still look forward to coming to the library every week," said Martin. "I've seen a lot of change since I first came here and that keeps my job fresh and exciting. I can't imagine not working for the library."

Volunteers have been giving service since the library was founded in 1908 and perform such functions as checking in returned library books, assisting with inventories, preparing materials for storytimes and other children's programs, covering bookjackets and preparing materials for the shelf, greeting library patrons, assisting with building upkeep and special building projects, and helping to support library promotion.

The library has many opportunities available and welcomes volunteers age twelve years or older. Interested persons may contact Sue Smith, director of volunteer services, to obtain further information or an application.

A more subtle but equally effective way to highlight your volunteers in the press is to be sure to include them in photos that you send to the paper to report on a program or event. Whenever a volunteer does appear in a library press photo, be sure that the caption includes the fact that "Sue Jones is a volunteer at the Anycity Public Library." You may wish to add emphasis to volunteer roles in the library by saying something like, "Pictured is Sue Jones, one of Anycity Public Library's 345 volunteers."

It seems as though everyone reads "Letters to the Editor." What a great place, then, to give credit to your volunteers for their efforts on the library's behalf. Whether you wish to bring attention to a special event made possible by volunteers (the shifting of a collection to new quarters, for example) or just to say thanks in general, a letter to the editor is an easy and effective way to do so. Naming names is especially nice, and if you are recognizing a small volunteer crew for a special project, it's probably possible to list each one. If you are just letting your world know how much you appreciate volunteers at the library, and if you have a large volunteer staff, naming names may not be feasible. Even if you can't mention each one by name, however, they are all likely to be very pleased by this gesture.

The city newspaper is not the only game in town. There are other avenues for public recognition as well. How about radio? If your library does not currently use the radio for Public Service Announcements (PSAs), open that door with one about volunteers at the library. Whether recruiting or giving recognition, a radio PSA is a wonderful way to reach the ears of many people in your community. Contact your local radio station manager and see if you can get special billing during National Volunteer Week. It may be that in addition to a special PSA (that the station may help you write), you can get yourself a guest slot on the radio to talk about your volunteers and the difference they make in the quality of service you provide. If you're interested in turning the occasion into a recruiting opportunity as well, bring a volunteer with you so that she can talk about why she is willing to give time to the library.

Don't forget your own press. Most libraries have some sort of house organ. Whether it's a monthly newsletter or a weekly calendar of events, use your own in-house publications to give recognition to your volunteers. You may, for example, want to have a special column devoted to a "Volunteer of the Month" telling a little about the volunteer—their background, hobbies, etc.; and telling something about the work they do for the library.

One caveat with this and other recognition programs, singling people out can often backfire in terms of morale. A volunteer who is *not* chosen for a special recognition but feels she should have been might feel that she is taken for granted and that would dampen the spirits of anyone. If volunteers are singled out, you might want to be sure to use objective criteria for doing so—length of service for example, or completion of a very special and complex task. If your volunteer workforce is fairly small, you could simply rotate volunteers receiving special recognition until you are sure each one has been profiled.

In-House Recognition

In addition to keeping volunteers and their contributions visible through the library's newsletter, you can highlight their service in other ways as well. For example, consider keeping a large wooden plaque in a highly visible location in the library to which brass name plates can be added. As a volunteer reaches a predetermined number of years of service, her name could be added to the plaque. Often we use this method to recognize members of the community for their financial support of library services, why not consider the years of service a volunteer gives as equally important? This kind of permanent recognition for volunteer contribution to library services will honor your long-time volunteers and give newer volunteers something to look forward to.

Another way to highlight your volunteers in-house is to put up a display that honors the work they do. Take pictures of each volunteer engaged in her library work and make a collage. Be sure to label each picture with the volunteer's name and perhaps with the department in which she works. Not only will this be a very visual reminder that the library benefits from volunteer services of community residents, it's a very personal way to give recognition. If yours is a large library with a correspondingly large volunteer force, such a pictorial display may work to introduce volunteers to each other who work at different times of the day or week. In fact, I know of one such display that revealed to a volunteer that her cousin also worked for the library and neither one knew it!

Occasional volunteer staff meetings are excellent for getting the word out simultaneously to all volunteers about changes in operations, procedures, and policies, but they can also serve as an opportunity to let your volunteers know that they are not taken for granted. Whenever you meet with volunteers to discuss library issues, remember to precede the meeting (and close it as well) with a strong statement about how much their services mean to you and the library staff. As well as making a general statement regarding your appreciation, be specific. Let them know how many hours of volunteer services the library enjoys each week. Let them know what services have been enhanced or maintained due to their efforts. Let everyone hear it at once. Never let an opportunity go by to foster the pride they feel in working for the library.

Don't overlook the simple importance of giving your volunteers special "Volunteer" buttons, badges or name-tags to wear during their shifts. Wearing the badge will make your volunteers stand out and because they are probably proud of their work in the library, they will be pleased with this simple form of recognition. In addition, if volunteers are readily identified as such, you will be subtly promoting your volunteer program and you will be signaling the public that a particular person *is* a volunteer and, therefore, will be able to provide only limited service.

Public Ceremony

In most cities and towns there is an opportunity to have the municipal government give formal recognition for special services or events. Many libraries, for example, have received a formal resolution from their city government in honor of National Library Week. Such recognition lends clout to our operations as well as visibility. Because everyone in the community benefits by volunteer services at the library, it should be easy to convince your municipal government to pass a resolution honoring the library's volunteer staff. Such a resolution should include the number of volunteers who work for the library as well as the number of total hours contributed during the past year.

Of course, any resolution is only as important as it is deemed by those who hear it so be sure that plenty of people know about it. Perhaps you could fill the council chambers with members of your paid and volunteer staff. What a great way to impress upon members of local government (the very people who fund the library) that the library is so important people enthusiastically give their time and talent to make it the very best it can be.

If you are able to make a public ceremony in recognition of library volunteers, be sure that the press is there to cover it. Let them know ahead of time that the city government has drafted a resolution to honor them. You will generate interest by the press if you send along a release telling about the various jobs accomplished by volunteers, the number of hours given by them, and listing the names of all volunteers who have worked for the library during the course of the year. Be sure when you attend the ceremony you bring a camera. Not only will you want to have pictures of the event for future displays, you will also want to ensure newspaper coverage that includes pictures and if the press doesn't show up, you'll have pictures to send them along with a follow-up press release and a copy of the formal resolution.

Finally, make a big deal of the resolution within the library. Have the resolution framed and then hang it right out front in the lobby where everyone is sure to see it. The resolution and the pride you show in hanging it will honor the volunteers and it will let them know that their service matters very much to you.

The "Great Idea" Award

Volunteers, of course, give libraries more than time. They contribute ideas as well—ideas that often come from a very different perspective than those of us who become so deeply ensconced in the forest we hardly remember what a tree even looks like. Admittedly not all ideas are tenable; sometimes only a few actually work out. Nevertheless, there is that occasional spark of innovation that can transform the way we traditionally do things.

When a volunteer does something that goes way beyond the call of duty or comes up with an idea that really is special, it makes sense to give them credit in a public way. A "Great Idea" award, or any award for special achievement, is a way of letting your volunteers know that they do have a valued voice in library operations, direction, and planning, and that their ideas and extra efforts really do make a difference.

It doesn't have to take a lot of effort to highlight a special contribution and the way in which you give such an award could vary significantly. It might be appropriate to take a humorous approach and give a gentle "roasting" to the person who came up with a great new idea—listing crazy fictitious ideas that this particular volunteer came up with first then abandoned before hitting the mark. Or, you might want to take the honor very seriously and include it as a part of an annual event giving a certificate, plaque or gift. Whatever you do, the volunteer will appreciate being recognized.

If given only on occasion, the award could well take on a special significance which will enhance its value to the recipient. And while singling out one volunteer can have some negative repercussions (see above), very special contributions to the library will be understood and applauded by everyone on staff.

Annual Events

At some point in the year, nearly every library that enjoys the services of volunteers, takes time out to thank them all in a very special way—with a party or event solely in their honor. Whether an annual volunteer luncheon, recognition dinner, a holiday potluck, or a complete day of festivities, an annual event to celebrate volunteers and the contributions they've made throughout the year will let all of them know how much they mean to you and the library staff and they give everyone a reason to get away from the daily grind and just have fun!

Volunteer Luncheons or Dinners

It's very common practice among libraries to honor volunteers with an annual luncheon or dinner. These events can be as fancy or "homespun" as you want and can afford. If funding isn't a big issue (and it needn't be—see "Funding for Volunteer Recognition," below), the type of celebration may depend more on the personality of your staff and volunteers than on anything else.

If you hope to make the occasion fun as well as using it as an opportunity to say thanks, you might want to get some members of your staff in on the planning. Formal lunches or dinners at the local banquet hall can be both stuffy and boring. The last thing you want to do is create a tradition that everyone attends out of duty. If you are truly interested in showing your appreciation, work to make the event something that everyone looks forward to every year.

If you would like to make the occasion something very special and memorable, you might consider hosting an evening of dinner and dancing, with a local band or small orchestra hired for the event. Such a night would give everyone the opportunity to get out and dust off those special evening clothes that we seldom have an opportunity to wear. If the evening is to be both special and formal, consider sending each of your volunteers a corsage or boutonniere with the library's compliments.

During the course of the evening, take some time for speeches. The president of the Board of Trustees could be prevailed upon to discuss the importance of volunteers in enhancing the quality of library services. If volunteers accomplished something special during the year (barcoding the collection, campaigning for a bond issue, working through a building project, for example), talk about it and thank them doubly for services well beyond the call of duty. If you do give out awards or certificates, this evening would be an ideal time to hand them out with personal thanks to each and every volunteer.

We've all been to events where the speeches go on and on while the fizzle leaves the champagne and the band dozes. Don't take the festivity out of the night with a lot of ritual. The volunteers do deserve recognition, however, and it's entirely appropriate and fitting that some special words of gratitude are expressed in a formal way. Then, let the fun begin!

Some library volunteer staffs would be much more comfortable with a more informal setting. A lunch at one of your city's best restaurants or even a pot-luck in the library's community room can be an excellent way to get together with all of your volunteers giving you a chance to thank them. If you decide on something like a pot-luck, be sure that it's the staff that does the cooking (and that staff members feel fine about doing so—after all it's not in their job descriptions) or have the lunch catered.

The staff can go a long way in making a luncheon special and memorable. It's likely that you know which staff members have a flair for comedy and theater. Put them in charge of entertainment for the event. I worked for a library once where two members on staff were true hams. Each year they worked together to come up with a skit that they egged the rest of the staff members into producing for the volunteers. The goal, of course, was to out-do both each other (in the idea department) and the previous year's performance. The skits, usually with the theme of what library services would be without volunteers, were extremely slapstick and silly; the staff members with varying degrees of thespian talents usually succeeded in looking ridiculous — and the volunteers loved it!

Over time, the entertainment took on a somewhat vaudevillian tone and had gained a modest reputation of its own throughout the community. I won't go so far as to say that people were lining up to volunteer at the library so that they could enjoy one of our annual presentations, but I do know that volunteers began asking well in advance of our annual luncheon what we were planning this year! I believe that adding such a personal touch to what might otherwise be a fairly stodgy occasion, increased our volunteers' sense of being truly appreciated and well liked.

If you do sponsor a luncheon or dinner to honor volunteers once a year, let your imagination play a part in determining what you'll do, where you'll eat, and how you will make the event memorable and *fun*. This is your thank-you to the volunteers, don't be satisfied that you've made the gesture, go the extra distance and create an event that people will remember long after it's over, and that they'll look forward to again next year.

A Day (or Week!) of Celebration

Not content with just a lunch or dinner once a year? Do you feel that your volunteers deserve more? Why not have a whole day (or even a whole week) of activities and programs designed to honor volunteers and to show the community at large how much they do for the library? A special "Volunteer Day" will give you a chance to show your appreciation in a variety of ways and it will also give your volunteer workforce the exposure they deserve.

National Volunteer Week often coincides with National Library Week (NLW) in April. What a great opportunity to combine your promotional efforts to celebrate both libraries and library volunteers! Planning will be streamlined if activities planned for NLW focus, at least in part, on library volunteers. The press coverage that you plan, can emphasize the service that volunteers give each week and with a dual agenda, you are likely to increase the attention local media is willing to pay to the event.

There are many ways in which you can highlight volunteers during a day or week-long event. Put pictures of your volunteers up around the library with their names and what it is they do. Print a big banner proclaiming that it's "Anycity Public Library Volunteer Day" and hang it in a very visible location. Make big volunteer buttons for those who will be working that day or week and hand out corsages. Tie a ribbon around those visible areas where volunteers make a contribution — your book carts, shelves, circulation area, display cases, for example. Whatever you can think of to do to show off volunteer services to your patrons should be incorporated into the plan.

Present some special programs for that week and introduce each one with a dedication to volunteers. A reading by the local theater group from books, essays or poems about libraries, reading, and books is a wonderful way to celebrate libraries and lends itself well to a special dedication or poem about volunteers. When you promote these events, promote them as being part of your library's celebration of volunteers and be sure that each of the volunteers on your staff gets a special invitation to attend.

You might plan a simple open-house for one evening where refreshments are served and the public is invited to come in and meet the library's volunteers. If you host an event like this, be sure that your Friends of the Library know about it and are invited (via their newsletter) and be sure that trustees make a special effort to be there. Send invitations to the mayor, the city manager and members of the city council so that they will have an opportunity to visit the library, meet volunteers, and offer their own appreciation. As simple and informal as these sorts of events are, it's amazing how well attended they can be especially if promoted well throughout the community.

Don't wait for the media to catch on. Let them know well in advance what you are planning. Send the local paper a schedule of events along with an invitation to attend. Contact the local radio station and ask if you can have some time during the course of the volunteer week or during the specially designated volunteer day to come and talk about volunteer services in the library. If you are planning special programs or events for this occasion, put posters and flyers up around town so that the event (and your volunteers) gets even more publicity. When it's all over, be sure and follow up with a press release that reports on the event and tells about volunteers in the library.

Planning a special day or week each year where you focus on contributions volunteers make will certainly let them know that they make a difference. In addition, all that attention is very likely to interest other people in the community in library work. Finally, such a public promotion will send the message that library is important enough to warrant the gift of time by people in the community and it will send the message that the library is managing its resources well by augmenting its operating budget with volunteer services.

Funding for Volunteer Recognition

While there are certain activities and gestures of appreciation you can make without spending much money, it is equally likely that you will want to do something special or give gifts and awards that will have to be funded. If you only need a small amount of money, or if your plans are being incorporated with normal library events, it may be that you are able to find money in the library's operating budget to support your plans. Hosting a lunch or dinner, giving gifts or flowers, printing up special certificates or handing out plaques, however, means finding money not allocated to you through the budget. Don't let that stifle your plans—there is money out there and honoring your volunteers is a good reason to find it.

Many libraries are able to fund special occasions and events through the Friends of the Library. If they haven't been approached in the past to sponsor a special volunteer event or support the printing of certificates or purchase of small gifts of appreciation, you should talk to them now. Friends and volunteers are natural allies and the Friends will understand well why it's important to honor volunteers.

Of course, it is entirely possible that the Friends' executive board might feel a bit of conflict because oftentimes members of the

Friends are also volunteers! This conflict shouldn't, however, be too troublesome if what you want them to fund is an *event* that will be shared by everyone rather than gifts or awards that may go only to someone who is also a member of the Friends' decision making body. Because, in fact, those who work for the Friends of the Library are also volunteering their time on behalf of the library, you should be sure that they are honored as well — even if they are funding the event.

Another very good avenue for possible funding is your local business community. If you have not already developed strong ties with your corporate community, this may be just the door to future relations and future support from them. Leaders of the business community will understand well the value of volunteers to the library and its service. Members of the business community also understand that a good library benefits them. Libraries enhance the quality of life in a community. They are an important part of the cultural and educational fabric that helps entice new people and business to move to the area. It should not be difficult, then, to convince local corporations and businesses that sponsorship of volunteer recognition events and awards is worthy of their support.

When you approach businesses or corporations for funding, it is important to let them know exactly what your plans are and why you feel what you are doing is important. Be specific. What will you be doing? What will it cost? How much sponsorship are you seeking from this particular business? Will you be asking for support from other businesses in the community as well? Go to them with any information you think they might want and with information that helps you make your case for support. You should be prepared to tell them how many volunteers work for the library, how many hours are contributed each year and how much that time would cost if incorporated in the library's budget. Let them know about the diversity of your volunteer staff and let them know the types of services they provide.

If you plan to do something extremely special (and expensive), you might consider going to a major corporation or business in your community and make a pitch for full sponsorship that would bring them visibility in the community as well. If you are able to find sponsorship from a particular business, invite the CEO to attend and perhaps make a short speech about the importance of volunteers in the community and the importance of the library. There is, I know, some reluctance among some librarians to bring the corporate world into the library fold and I understand and respect the reasons for the reluctance. Remember, though, that businesses and corporations are part of the community too and remember that they can be powerful allies for the library.

When a business or corporation makes a financial contribution to the library they are literally "buying into" the library and its mission. You have a perfect opportunity to invite them to add their appreciation for the services volunteers give to the library when you approach them for support of a special event in their honor. If presented well, your request will likely be viewed as a very attractive opportunity for a business to show its support for such a popular institution as the library and such a noble cause as honoring those who donate their time to it. It is likely that if these events become a tradition, you will have local businesses and corporations coming to you with their willingness to provide financial support!

Simple Gestures of Appreciation

In the end, the most valuable way to show your appreciation to those who volunteer is to ensure that they never feel their services are taken for granted. Special events and awards are wonderful and as simple as a certificate of appreciation may seem to us, to them it means that we've noticed their contributions and that we have taken the time to formalize our appreciation. It's not the certificate necessarily, it's the gesture.

All the big events and special awards we can devise however, will not make up for a negligent attitude throughout the year. The importance of simply saying "thank you" at the end of a volunteer's workshift can't be overemphasized. In my very first library job, I remember a volunteer who would walk to our small library during the worst winter blizzards when everything else was closed down, the streets nearly impassable, and when no other staff members were able to get in (including the director and myself!). Mary had a key and she would make her way in so that she would be available to answer the phone and check books out to the more adventurous souls in our community.

I asked Mary why she would do it when it was completely understandable for the library to be closed and when, often, she wasn't even scheduled to work. "I do it for Patty [the director]," she told me. "Since the day she came, Patty has never failed to tell me 'Thank you' at the end of my shift, letting me know how much my volunteer work means to her. Coming in when no one else can is my way of saying 'Thank you' to Patty!"

I was glad that I learned this valuable lesson so early in my career. Volunteers aren't in it for the certificates, the plaques, the lunches, the dinners, or even for locally renowned entertainment by the staff! Volunteers work for the library because they want to do something that makes a difference for an agency they believe in. At most, what they require in return is simple and genuine feedback from the staff that their being at the library does, indeed, make a difference.

Bibliography

Caywood, Carolyn. "Compulsory Volunteerism," *School Library Journal,* vol. 38 (November 1992), p. 46.

In reaction to a Maryland state law mandating that teens give 75 hours of volunteer service in order to receive a high school diploma, Caywood points out that if volunteers do not work by *choice*, they cheapen the experience for the rest who do. Praising the teens who freely give their time to the library, Caywood points out that the library does not want teen volunteers who come simply at the behest of their parents saying, "we do not want the library to become synonymous with drudgery or punishment."

In contrast to those who come to the library because they must fulfill a requirement, teen volunteers in Caywood's Bayside Area Public Library (Virginia), freely choose to give an estimated 30 hours per year, enhancing the library's annual book sale, working in the circulation area, and even fighting the battle against library budget cuts! This spirit of support, says Caywood, would be jeopardized with a significant increase of those who are there only because they have to be.

Chadbourne, Robert. "Volunteers in the Library: Both Sides Must Give in Order to Get," *Wilson Library Bulletin,* (June 1993), pp. 26–27.

This article, which focuses on the development of a volunteer staff at the Newton (Massachusetts) Free Library, gives a concise summary of both the perils and rewards of volunteers in libraries. Among potential problems outlined are issues of workers' compensation and liability, a shrinking volunteer pool, the possible threat to paid staff, and the problem of holding volunteers accountable. These potential problems, however, can be circumvented to a large extent according to Virginia Tashjian of the Newton Free Library.

In order to develop a viable volunteer work-force, Newton "appointed a staff coordinator, compiled a list of local organizations, drew a member from each, plus one from the Friends groups as an advisory committee, sent members out to recruit, and compiled a ten-item volunteer program guide."

Included in this informative article is discussion of how a volunteer force fits in with and is viewed by unions representing library staff. According to Diane Fay, president of Local 1526, American Federation of State, County and Municipal Employees, "Unions feel volunteer programs are useful as long as they are additional, but when the functioning of a library becomes dependent on volunteers, unions change their views."

Childs, Catherine C. and John Waite Bowers. "Cunning Passages, Contrived Corridors: Mobilizing Volunteers for a Public Library Tour," *Public Libraries*, vol. 32, no. 3 (May/June 1993), pp. 143–147.

Although this article was specifically written to share information and insight into developing a volunteer force to give guided tours of a new library, the information is easily transferrable to developing a force for any special project that will require many volunteers. Included are tips for developing a "reverse time line" to recruit and train volunteers, and the development of a manual to be used with volunteers during the training process.

The reverse time line is used to "transform an amorphous task into a specific, manageable series of subtasks." The manual was written to define the goal of the project, outline procedures for meeting the goal, encourage volunteers to "be yoursel(ves)—warm, intelligent, well informed, communicative," and to articulate expected results. Because the development and description of the recruiting process, time line, and manual are so clearly described in this article, it provides helpful guidance for anyone taking on the organization of a special volunteer project.

Clarke, Susan and others in *The Book Report*, vol. 11, no. 3. (November/December 1992) pp. 14–19.

This collection of brief articles in *The Book Report* center around the theme, "How to recruit, train and keep library volunteers of all ages" and includes helpful tips on all aspects of managing a volunteer work force. Although the articles address those issues relating to volunteers in school libraries, the information provided would be helpful for libraries of all types. Susan Clarke's article, for example, gives advice to those libraries that do not currently use volunteer services and strongly encourages them to establish a philosophy regarding library volunteers *before* bringing volunteers on board so that all policies and procedures will flow from that central philosophy.

In another article, Sally G. Weber talks about the important role a Friends group can play in both the development and the management of a volunteer work force, and how the group itself can be a valuable source of volunteers. Also included in this issue are ideas for scheduling volunteers, evaluating their performance and ways to encourage volunteers from all age groups.

Coles, Robert. *The Call of Service: A Witness to Idealism.* New York: Houghton Mifflin Company, 1993. 306p.

In his introduction, Coles says, "I am writing this book to explore the 'service' we offer to others and, not incidentally, to ourselves. I am hoping to document the subjectivity, the phenomenology of service: the many ways such activity is rendered; the many rationales, impulses, and values served in the implementation of a particular effort. . . . I am hoping as well to discuss the connections between community service and intellectual reflection."

This book, which focuses primarily on volunteer services to the disadvantaged, is a deeply thoughtful investigation of what motivates people to give of themselves; to make the world a better place for others. In addition to the obligation many feel to give back to their community, is the often repeated sentiment expressed by one woman who spent her life taking care of people in Harlem. She said she did herself "a lot of good [by] doing good."

But beyond all the expressed reasons, there exists throughout the book an inexpressible spirit compelling people to go beyond their own needs and give service to others. Coles' own father expresses his volunteer work as an act of faith (as Coles interprets it). When queried as to his own motivation he says, "I frankly doubt I could continue [volunteer activity] if I looked too hard within."

Managing volunteers successfully means understanding them as human beings and understanding, to whatever degree possible, what motivates people to give their time. Coles' work is important both for a better understanding of volunteerism in America, and for celebrating it.

Gerhardt, Lillian N. "Three Little Words," *School Library Journal*, vol. 37 (November 1991), p. 4.

Gerhardt, while praising volunteers' ability to "alleviate" social ills though certainly not to "eradicate" them, cautions the importance of drawing the line between volunteer and professional. Gerhardt tells of the Stockton-San Joaquin County (California) Public Library's budget cuts and an administrator's reassurance to the public that no reductions in service would be forthcoming because volunteers would simply step in for the laid-off professional librarians. Gerhardt points out the absurdity of replacing professionals with "a shrinking corps of volunteers for local public services, such as hospitals — where the casual assumption of the title 'doctor' could land a volunteer in the slammer."

Hayghe, Howard V. "Volunteers in the U.S.: Who Donates the Time?" *Monthly Labor Review*, vol. 114, no. 2 (February 1991), pp. 17–23.

This article is based on the May 1989 Current Population Survey (a monthly sample survey conducted by the Bureau of the Census for the Bureau of Labor Statistics) which reported that 38 million people volunteered for work without pay sometime during the reporting year ending in May 1989. A demographic breakdown showing the groups that are most and least likely to volunteer is included as is a comparative study with two previous Current Population Study findings regarding volunteerism (one in 1965 and another in 1974).

In addition to the astounding number of people who engaged in some kind of volunteer activity in 1989 (the equivalent of 1 in 5 adults 16 years and over), is the equally impressive statistic that of those volunteering, nearly 30 percent do some kind of volunteer work every week. Also included in the report is the fact that those in the 35–44 year age group give the most volunteer hours — not the over 65 group that many would have predicted. More predictable, however, is the fact that higher education equates with higher number of volunteer hours given as does income, gender (female), and race (white).

McCune, Bonnie. "The New Volunteerism: Making It Pay Off for Your Library," *American Libraries*, vol. 24, no. 9 (October, 1993) pp. 822–824.

Using the growth and success of the Denver Public Library's Volunteer Services, McCune focuses on ways to develop library volunteer work forces. Among the DPL's successful strategies described in this article are active recruitment of "nontraditional" volunteers (including court diversion candidates, and members of minority groups), including the business community in the recruitment of volunteers, and offering young people the opportunity to learn through volunteer services.

Also discussed in the article is the importance of collaborating with other organizations using volunteers for training and support and using other organizations or businesses as volunteers for special projects—in Denver's case, for example, Coors Brewing Company employees provided volunteer staff for their annual book sale.

Key in the development of successful volunteer work force, according to McCune, is a willingness by the library to be flexible with regard to potential volunteer requirements which she points out, have changed dramatically over the years.

Wells, Linda Bennett and Alice Bennett Ihrig. "Volunteers in the Library: The Role of Trustees" in *The Library Trustee: A Practical Guidebook*, 4th edition. Chicago: American Library Association, 1988. pp. 144–151.

Written for trustees in order to give an overview of how volunteers fit into the library's staff, this article gives good solid information on why volunteers are valuable, under what circumstances libraries should *not* use volunteers, why trustees should not, simultaneously, be volunteers at the library (stating clearly that the "chain of command" for staff must also apply for volunteers), the importance of written policies with regard to volunteer programs, evaluation and recognition of volunteers, and why volunteers make good library advocates.

Ihrig, especially, is an established authority on library trustees and this article is an unabashed endorsement of the value of volunteers. Any librarian, therefore, who is having trouble convincing trustees to authorize the creation of a volunteer staff, or needs to bolster a request to trustees to support funding for a volunteer coordinator, would do well to introduce this article (and book) to the board.

White, Herbert S. "The Double-Edged Sword of Library Volunteerism," *Library Journal*, vol. 118 (April 15, 1993), pp. 66–67.

White clearly brings into focus the issue of using volunteers in place of paid professional staff. While recognizing that the use of volunteers "is a crucial and honored one," he goes on to stress that without clearly defining the limits of volunteer roles in libraries, libraries themselves are at risk. White says, "If it is possible to stop funding libraries but still claim to have them [because they are being "run" by volunteers], the decision is no longer painful; it is absurdly simple."

White's article makes a passionate case for the critical importance of excellent volunteer training which includes clear job descriptions and limits of responsibility that are spelled out and enforced.

Index